THE

WEIGHT TRAINING

WORKBOOK

BY JIM BENNETT

- THE BASICS OF WEIGHT TRAINING
- STRETCHING EXERCISES
- ABDOMINAL EXERCISES
- CHEST EXERCISES
- TRICEP EXERCISES
- BICEP EXERCISES
- FOREARM EXERCISES
- BACK EXERCISES
- SHOULDER EXERCISES
- LEG EXERCISES
- CALF EXERCISES
- WEIGHT TRAINING RECORDS

JBBA Publishing • Appleton, Wisconsin

Published by JBBA Publishing, Inc.
Post Office Box 842
Appleton, Wisconsin 54912-0842
800-245-7897

Illustrations by Tom Yessis, James Furnner,
and David Kacmarynski

Manufactured in the United States of America
Printed by Neenah Printing

ISBN: 1-879031-00-0

INTRODUCTION

Congratulations on your decision to become involved in weight training. To be successful in weight training, it is important to develop an understanding of all aspects of the activity. Understanding the basic principles of weight training will allow you to establish and maintain a high quality, life-long weight training program that will yield maximum results.

It is also important to become knowledgeable with all the weight training exercises, how to properly perform them, muscle groups involved and correct technique and form. Most persons will watch someone performing an exercise they are not familiar with and then attempt to perform the same exercise themselves. This is often referred to as "Monkey See – Monkey Do." "The Weight Training Workbook" was developed for use while working out to provide you with easy to understand information on weight training and how to correctly perform popular exercises.

"The Weight Training Workbook" contains pages for recording your short- and long-term training objectives, monthly changes in measurements and daily workouts. The changes you want to take place in your body will not come overnight. If you do not possess an understanding of the principles of weight training or the amount of time it takes for your body to respond to the new demands being placed on it, you can fall short of your expectations.

To achieve the results you desire you first need to record your training objectives. If they are realistic and attainable you will have no trouble achieving them. A measurement record has been provided to record your monthly changes in body measurements and is designed to establish monthly goals. This will give you something to work towards each month which will add to your incentive to stay with your weight training program.

The pages for recording your daily workouts will allow you to realize progress made toward your anticipated goals. On each page you can maintain an accurate record of the number of sets, reps and weights used and note any factors that may have influenced your workout. Looking back after the first few months you will be able to see the progress you have made and determine which exercises or techniques have yielded the best results.

I encourage you to stick to your decision to become involved in weight training and hope that one day you will achieve your long- term training objectives. Its well worth the effort!

Best wishes with your weight training.

Jim Bennett

CONTENTS

1 The Basics of Weight Training . . . 11

Weight Training Defined 11
The Weight Training Environment 12
Clothing 13
Establishing Your Weight Training Objectives 14
Losing Weight And Inches 15
Gaining Weight And Building Mass 15
Weight Training And Aerobic Endurance 16
Muscle Strength And Endurance 16
A Training Partner 17
"No Pain – No Gain" 17
Drinking Water 19
Weight Training Safety 20
The Eight Basic Principles Of Weight Training 23
Weight Training Intensity 26
Beginning A Weight Training Routine 26
Reps and Sets 27
Varying Your Weight Training Program 28
Resting Between Sets 28
Proper Form 29
Breathing 29
Recovering From A Workout 30
Split Routines 30
Advanced Weight Training 32
Overtraining 34
Saunas And Steambaths 36
Weight Training Myths 38

2 Stretching Exercises . . . 39

Alternate Toe Touches 40
Calf Stretches 41
Feet Apart Forward Bends 42
Forward Bends 43
Inner Thigh Stretch 44
Quadriceps Stretch 46
Shoulder Stretch 45
Side Bends 47
Spinal Twists 48

3 Abdominal Exercises . . . 49

Alternate Knee Raises 50
Bent-Knee Hanging Leg Raises 51
Bent-Knee Vertical Leg Raises 52
Bent-Over Twists 53
Crunches 54
Flat Bench Leg Raises 55
Hanging Leg Raises 56
Jack Knives 57
Reverse Trunk Twists 58
Roman Chair Sit-Ups 59
Sit-Ups 60
Twisting Crunches 61
Twisting Sit-Ups 62

4 Chest Exercises . . . 63

Bench Press 64
Bent-Arm Pullovers 65
Cable Crossovers 66
Decline Bench Press 67
Dips 68
Dumbbell Bench Press 69
Dumbbell Flyes 70
Incline Bench Press 71
Incline Dumbbell Flyes 72
Pec Dec 73

5 Tricep Exercises . . . 75

Dips Behind Back 76
Dumbbell Kickbacks 77
Lying Cross Face Tricep Ext. 78
Lying Tricep Extension 79
One-Arm Tricep Ext. 80
Seated Tricep Ext. 81
Tricep Pushdowns 82

6 Bicep Exercises . . . 83

Alternate Dumbbell Curl 84
Bicep Machine Curl 85
Concentration Curl 86
Hammer Curl 87
Incline Dumbbell Curl 88
Preacher Curl 89
Pulley Curl 90
Reverse Bicep Curl 91
Seated Dumbbell Curl 92

7 Forearm Exercises . . . 93

Barbell Wrist Curl 94
Behind The Back Wrist Curl 95
Dumbbell One-Arm Wrist Curl 96
Reverse Wrist Curl 97
Wrist Curl 98

8 Back Exercises . . . 99

Barbell Bent-Over Row 100
Bent-Over Dumbbell Rows 101
Dumbbell Shrug 102
Good Morning 103
Hyperextension 104
Lat Pulldown To Chest 105

Narrow Grip Lat Pulldown 106
Seated Pulley Rowing 107
Straight-Arm Pullover 108
T-Bar Bent-Over Row 109
Upright Row 110
Wide-Grip Chin 111

9 Shoulder Exercises . . . 113

Arnold Press 114
Behind The Neck Press 115
Bent-Over Cable Lateral 116
Dumbbell Press 117
Front Raises 118

One-Arm Cross Cable Lateral 119
Overhead/Military Press 120
Prone Lateral Raise 121
Seated Bent-Over Lateral 122
Side lateral Raises 123

10 Leg Exercises . . . 125

Deadlifts 126
Front Squat 127
Hack Squat 128
Leg Abduction 129
Leg Adduction 130

Leg Curl 131
Leg Extension 132
Leg Press 133
Lunges 134
Squat 135

11 Calf Exercises . . . 137

Calf Raises 138
Donkey Calf Raises 139
Reverse Calf Raises 140

Seated Calf Raises 141
Standing Calf Raises 142

12 Weight Training Records . . . 143

Short-Term Goals 144
Long-Term Goals 145
Measurement Record 146-147
Daily Weight Training Records 148

1
THE BASICS OF WEIGHT TRAINING

Weight Training Defined

Weight training is defined as progressive resistance exercise. This is a form of muscular exercise using resistance provided by barbells and dumbbells (free weights), or exercise machines to stimulate muscle growth and increase muscle strength and endurance. A weight training program consists of a series of different exercises grouped together by sets and repetitions. Repetitions (reps) are the number of complete and continuous executions of an exercise. Sets are the distinct groupings of repetitions performed.

The term weight training can been divided into four specific types of resistance exercise.

Bodybuilding — The objective of the bodybuilder is to change the appearance of his or her body by exercising with progressively heavier weights. This type of weight training program will allow the reduction of body areas while strengthening and increasing the size of specific muscle groups. Bodybuilding has gained increased popularity as a competitive sport for both men and women. For some, bodybuilding is a means of losing weight and inches, for others it's a means of gaining weight and building muscle size and strength.

Olympic Lifting — In this division both men and women compete to lift the heaviest weight for one single repetition in a required exercise.

Sport Specific Training — Sport specific training is used by athletes to increase muscular strength and endurance. This form of overall conditioning will normally allow the athlete to improve in his or her specific sport.

Injury Rehabilitation — Weight training has been recognized by sports medicine experts as a method of recovery from injury-weakened joints and muscles. Once the initial injury has healed, a prescribed weight training program can help strengthen damaged muscles and joints.

Now that you are familiar with the four divisions of weight training you can ask yourself, *"where do I fit in?"* If you are not recovering from an injury, trying to improve your performance in a specific sport, or training for Olympic lifting, you are simply bodybuilding. If your ambition is to lose weight and inches, or gain weight and build muscle, you are involved in a form of bodybuilding. For women it is often called "bodysculpting."

The Weight Training Environment

There are two options available when it comes to deciding where to workout. The first option is your home. There is a wide selection of fitness equipment designed specifically for home use. If this is your decision, thoroughly research the advantages and disadvantages of each manufacturer. You will want to perform several exercises for each major muscle group.

Your second option is to join a commercial gym or health club. This also includes schools, colleges, and YMCA's. When shopping for a heath club or gym be sure to check certification. If a health club or gym advertises it has trained, qualified or certified instructors, ask to look at their certification. If they try to skirt the issue, move on. A well managed health club or gym will have certified staff ready to answer all your questions, especially if you are a new member with little or no understanding of weight training. Since cost is a major factor when purchasing a health club or gym membership, be sure to perform a through inspection. Inspect equipment for proper maintenance, locker rooms and showers for cleanliness, catch racks and collars for barbells, and rooms for good ventilation/air conditioning. The final step in your inspection is to ask the current members what they feel is good about their health club or gym. When it passes your inspection and you feel confident about the staff and type of membership offered, then sign your check and prepare to begin weight training.

Clothing

Your weight training environment will dictate the type of clothing to be worn. Weight training is normally performed indoors so there will be specific guidelines to be followed concerning proper workout apparel. When deciding what to wear, keep in mind that it must be loose-fitting and elastic enough to allow movement through a full range of motion. Clothing should be comfortable as you do not want to become restricted during your movements.

Today's selection of workout apparel includes all styles and designs, therefore you should have no problem finding something right for you. With many health clubs and gyms becoming co-ed, you will need to check if there are special clothing guidelines to be followed. I suggest that you consult with your club or gym before making a major purchase.

Establishing Your
Weight Training Objectives

It is important that your weight training program have a well planned objective and purpose. Before beginning it is important to determine your short- and long-term training objectives or goals. Whether it be to lose weight and inches, gain weight and build, or establish and maintain a high level of physical fitness, you will need to have your training objectives clearly laid out. It is highly recommended before your first workout that you consult with your physician concerning your desire to become involved in weight training. If your training objectives are realistic and attainable, your physician will give you the go-ahead that will increase your incentive to start your weight training program without hesitation.

Your decision to begin weight training should be a life-long commitment and not just a stray impulse. As with most people who become involved in weight training, there are a number of things about yourself you would like to change. I want to stress that your health, weight, and size will not change in a few weeks. The daily changes will be too small to observe, but after a few months you will be able to see progress being made toward your goals. This is why it is important to maintain an accurate record of your weight training workouts. By recording your efforts you will be able to look back over a period of time and realize significant progress being made toward your often evasive goals. This will provide you with the enthusiasm and determination to stick to your initial weight training objectives. When you have exhausted the daily weight training records in the workbook you can use "The Weight Training Record" to maintain an accurate record of your daily workouts. "The Weight Training Record" contains imporatant reference information found in the workbook, plus pages for recording your training objectives, monthly measurements and up to one year of daily workouts.

Losing Weight And Inches

The method by which you lose weight and inches is very simple: become involved in a regular aerobic exercise program and develop an understanding of the foods you frequently eat. These are the only two building blocks that can produce a lean, healthy, functional, vibrant and vigorous body. Fad diets, crash diets, fasting or whatever pills are currently being advertised will not provide you with the results you can achieve by understanding your eating habits and becoming involved in a regular aerobic exercise program.

A great way to develop an understanding of the foods you frequently eat and maintain a daily record of calories consumed to maintain your present weight or reach your ideal weight is with "The Weight Training Calorie Register." Ordering information can be found in the back of the workbook.

Gaining Weight And Building Mass

While one person is trying to lose weight and inches, another may be trying to gain weight and build muscle size, strength and endurance. Again, it is very simple. Proper diet and progressive resistance exercise are the only two building blocks that will allow you to attain the results you desire. Using progressively heavier weights during your workouts will promote increased muscle size and strength as your body adapts to the new demands being placed on it. Along with working your muscles harder than they have been accustomed to, it will be necessary to modify your diet to include foods which will promote muscle recovery and growth.

Weight Training
And Aerobic Endurance

Weight training (anaerobic activity) alone will not improve your aerobic endurance. Rather, weight training combined with an aerobic exercise class, running, cycling, swimming, skipping rope, climbing, or some other form of aerobic activity, will significantly improve your overall aerobic health. Aerobic exercise is defined as an activity that stimulates heart and lung activity producing beneficial changes in the body. The duration of the exercise can be from 20-30 minutes for high impact and up to 45-60 minutes for low impact aerobics. Aerobic exercise will promote fat reduction, improve stress tolerance and lower your blood pressure.

Muscle Strength
And Endurance

To achieve the full benefit from weight training it is necessary to develop and maintain a well-rounded program that exercises all the major muscle groups of the body. Muscle strength and endurance can only be developed by the overload principle. This is accomplished by increasing the amount of weight used or frequency and duration of sets and reps. Muscular strength is best developed by using heavy weights and performing a minimum number of repetitions. Muscle endurance is developed by using lighter weights and performing a greater number of repetitions. To some extent, muscular strength and endurance are developed using each method, but each favors a more specific development. The intensity of your weight training can be changed by varying the amount of weight used, repetitions performed, rest interval between sets and number of sets completed. To gain improvement in both muscular strength and endurance, most experts recommend 8-12 repetitions per set.

Any degree of overload will result in strength development, but performing reps at or near your maximum will provide the greatest gains in strength. Your expected gains are limited to your initial level of strength and potential for improvement. To achieve the greatest gains, keep your routine rhythmical, performed at a moderate to slow speed, and for maximum benefit always perform the exercise through its full range of motion.

The combination of frequency, intensity, and duration of exercise is the most effective method for producing successful results. The interaction of these variables provide the overload stimulus required for increased muscle strength and endurance.

A Training Partner

One way to get the most out of your weight training is to have a training partner. You are likely to meet old friends or make new acquaintances that have the same training objectives as you. Most people will invite the idea of a training partner. Be selective though – you want to train with someone who can provide additional enthusiasm and incentive to get the most out of your workouts.

Having a training partner is the best way to stay on track with your weight training program. You are less likely to miss a workout if you know someone is expecting you at the health club or gym at a certain time. A training partner can make your workouts more stimulating and enjoyable.

"No Pain – No Gain"

The expression *"No Pain – No Gain"* became prevalent in the fifties and has held its ground to this day. Athletes were often driven by their coaches to perform at or above their peak performance level and were taught that pain, either physical or psychological, was an indication of work output. Driving one's self to such a level of pain may be the motive of the well developed bodybuilder or powerlifter, but is not the case for the average person involved in weight training. Significant gains are attainable without subjecting yourself to this type of pain. This can cause possible injury.

Weight training is the ideal activity to stimulate the anaerobic metabolic process. The discomfort experienced in your muscles is a result of the by-products of anaerobic metabolism. The chief fuels used in anaerobic metabolism are glucose and glycogen. As a result of the breakdown of these fuels, "fatigue acids" (lactic and pyruvic) are produced. It is only when these acids reach a critical level that they irritate nerve endings close to the muscle fibers. This irritation is what causes muscle discomfort. It is through this biochemical process that muscle growth is stimulated.

It is important to become aware of and know the difference between discomfort and pain. Not all pain experienced is a positive sign of maximum muscle stimulation. Duration of pain is one of the primary ways of distinguishing between the two. The discomfort experienced with anaerobic metabolism is normally short in duration.

Your body will begin to produce natural chemicals known as "buffers" in an attempt to reduce the acidity. Thus, the discomfort experienced with weight training will normally subside within one to three days, depending on the intensity of the workout. Pain that does not subside after a few days is usually an indication of a possible muscle pull, strain, sprain, or tendon/ligament damage. In most cases, this type of pain will become more acute and intense. If this should happen, it is recommended that you stop training and consult your physician. Treatments for such pain will include rest, cold compress and elevation of the injured body part.

When pain is experienced while weight training and does not rapidly diminish during your rest period between sets, something is pathologically wrong and should be examined before proceeding with your weight training. If it is taking longer than it should for your muscles to recover after a workout, this might be due, in part, to your circulatory system. Only the circulatory system can deliver and distribute the nutrients required for muscle growth and remove waste products produced by regular weight training. Without a healthy circulatory system, your body will have difficulty coping with the new demands being placed upon it, stressing it beyond its functional capabilities.

Drinking Water

Proper nutrition begins with drinking 10-12, 8 oz. glasses of water each day, exclusive of any other liquid. When your body is in water balance it will:

1. Metabolize stored fat more efficiently.

2. Flush out waste products, including those resulting from fat metabolism.

3. Suppress the appetite to some extent.

4. Rid the body of fluid retention – retained water in the body shows up as excess weight.

5. Enhance overall muscle tone and size (muscles are roughly 85% water).

6. Lubricate body joints.

7. Tone up the skin and improve the complexion.

When you are involved in strenuous activities such as weight training or aerobic exercise you will lose a lot of water through sweating. If it is not replaced with sufficient water, dehydration can occur.

Another factor to consider when you do not drink enough water, is that your body will retain what water it has as a defense against dehydration. This retained water is often toxic, as the kidneys can not produce sufficient urine to properly detoxify the body. Therefore, the more water you drink, the less water your body will retain.

The amount of water you need to be in water balance will depend on your climate (you need more water in summer than winter); level of activity (the more you exercise, the more water you need); your weight (lighter people need less water than heavier people); and type of diet you are on (people who eat meat need more water than people who eat primarily fruits and vegetables).

Weight Training Safety

Weight training is only as safe as the person involved. When an individual does not follow proper safety procedures, he or she, along with other people nearby, become candidates for injury. For this reason, you need to become familiar with the following safety rules of weight training:

Have someone spot you. Always have someone spot you when using heavy weights such as when bench pressing or squatting. If you can not complete a rep, you will discover yourself in a precarious situation all by yourself. If you are unsure about your ability, ask someone to spot you. Your spotter will provide the additional enthusiasm needed to push up that last rep.

Never train alone. This is extremely important when weight training at home or in a health club or gym with few people around. Make sure someone is aware of your activities and ask them to check on you periodically.

Use catch racks. Health clubs and gyms should have catch racks available to perform heavy movements such as bench pressing and squatting. When used properly, they will prevent an errant barbell from causing injury to you and others.

Use collars. Collars are metal clamps placed on the ends of a barbell to prevent the weight plates from sliding off when performing an exercise. If your club or gym does not have collars available, insist that they get some.

Never hold your breath. Holding your breath will limit the oxygen flow to and from your brain. If held too long, it could cause you to black out. You could be seriously injured if this is experienced during your set.

Replace equipment where it belongs. When you finish performing your particular exercise always return weight plates, dumbbells, and barbells to their appropriate rack. Leaving them on the floor or propped up against a wall will only be setting someone up for possible injury. When the equipment is returned to its proper place, you will not have to search the club or gym for that one missing item. This is just common courtesy.

Train under competent supervision. If your health club or gym advertises they have trained, certified instructors on staff, by all means, make good use of them. I have often witnessed a new health club or gym member working out with no supervision; risking possible injury. Most persons will watch someone else performing an exercise they are not familiar with and then attempt to perform the same exercise themselves. This could cause possible injury as you do not understand the exercise and the person you are watching may not be performing the exercise correctly. This is often referred to as "Monkey

See – Monkey Do." A certified instructor will prevent the development of bad habits and possible injury.

Always warm-up before and cool-down after your weight training program. It is not smart to begin weight training without a proper warm-up as you can subject yourself to possible injury. A proper warm-up will increase you pulse rate, overall body temperature, blood and oxygen flow to specific muscles, and mentally prepare you for your weight training session.

There are two types of warm-up programs, *general* and *specific*. The general warm-up includes large muscle activities such as aerobics, jogging, skipping rope, stationary cycling, and stretching, and should last 10-15 minutes.

The specific warm-up follows the general warm-up in all exercise programs and consists of performing 2-3 light, but progressively heavier sets prior to training with heavy weights.

The cool-down immediately follows your weight training program and should last 5-15 minutes. This will allow your body to recover from your weight training session and begin to cool down. The cool-down will use the same activities as the general warm-up, but at a more casual pace, like easy jogging, stretching, and stationary cycling.

When performing demanding exercises, always wear a weight lifting belt. Weight lifting belts are made of leather and come in a variety of widths and thicknesses. A weight lifting belt will protect your abdominals and back from possible injury when performing movements with heavy weights. A weight lifting belt should be worn when performing demanding exercises such as the squat, and deadlifts.

Note: Wearing a tightly cinched lifting belt when performing other than demanding exercises can significantly raise your blood pressure.

Eight Basic Principles
Of Weight Training

Weight training programs are individualized and designed according to your particular anatomy, physiological condition and goals. Since no two persons have the same body type, height or weight, they stand little chance of attaining the same results if they train identically. So how do you determine which is the best weight training program? The answer lies in understanding and applying the eight basic principles of weight training and evaluating their effects. These basic principles apply to everyone, but how each principle is applied will depend on you.

1. Overload — This principle is defined as increasing the resistance to movement or frequency and duration of activity. When you want to promote increased muscle growth, strength and endurance you must go above and beyond what your muscles have grown accustomed to. Without overloading your muscles, it will be impossible to realize any gains. The four methods used to overload muscles are:

1. Increasing the resistance.
2. Increasing the number of repetitions.
3. Increasing the rate of work.
4. Increasing the amount of work in the same time period.

Each method is different and should be included in your training program, with the percentages of each varying according to your training objectives.

In general, increasing the resistance will promote increased muscle mass and strength; increasing the number of repetitions performed will promote improved muscular endurance; increasing the rate of work will give you more power; and increasing the amount of work performed will allow you greater gains in your overall strength and endurance.

Note: Too much of an increase can result in overtraining.

2. Universality — This is defined as the all-around development principle. You must develop muscle strength and endurance together with all the major muscles, joints and support structures. Universality will serve as a base for high intensity, specialized training and development which is essential for competitive bodybuilding and other sports.

3. Gradualness — The demands placed on your muscles must progress gradually in both volume and intensity. Physical ability and immediate level of fitness will determine your rate of increase. There is a law of nature that will not allow you to realize significant improvement in a short period of time. The only way to achieve long-lasting results is to adhere to gradualness. This can not be over emphasized. If you reach a plateau in your weight training, do not become alarmed. It may be an indication that you need to vary one or more of these eight weight training principles.

4. Progressiveness — This principle is closely related to gradualness and overload. When stimulating muscle to adapt to greater workloads, over a period of time there must be an increase in the amount of weight used. This weight increase will be greater when beginning weight training and become less when muscles become more developed.

5. Repetition — Performing repetitions with light to moderate weight is the only way to learn how to properly perform an exercise and provoke certain physiological changes to take place in your body. When learning how to correctly perform an exercise, performing repetitions will allow you to develop the proper technique.

If you start out using heavy weights, you will discover it impossible to learn correct technique. When your technique is faulty, you will not be working the muscle properly. This can lead to possible injury.

6. Consistency — If you are to realize any change in your weight and body measurements, you must commit yourself to a regular weight training schedule, the minimum being two times a week. Your body will respond only when exercises are repeated on a regular basis. This is where you come face to face with your commitment to improve your health and fitness. If you want results, you will have to stick to your weight training program.

7. Individualism — Your health, age, sex, and level of fitness will determine how well you can perform certain exercises. If you are in your mid-teens, elderly, or in poor physical health, using light weights and performing 8-12 repetitions is advisable. This will allow you to slowly work into your weight training program without subjecting your-self to possible injury.

8. Awareness — To be successful in weight training it is necessary to become aware of the why and wherefore of everything you do. This is the part of your weight training program that will generate the enthusiasm and desire to make it a permanent part of your lifestyle.

It is important to understand and vary these eight weight training principles to fit your weight training program. Possessing the knowledge and understanding of weight training, along with different methods and techniques used will ensure proper development of particular muscle groups and will bring you maximum results.

Weight Training Intensity

The intensity of your weight training will depend entirely upon your present level of fitness. Weight training subjects your muscles to a load greater than they have known and will provoke a soreness you are not accustomed to. To prevent severe muscle discomfort, gradually introduce your muscles to the new demands. Any major and/or minor discomfort can be avoided when you follow a gradual weight training program during the first 4-6 weeks. Your initial training will consist of performing 1-3 light sets of each exercise during the first few months. From there you will gradually add sets and weight to your training program until you experience little or no soreness.

Beginning A Weight Training Routine

The beginner who wants to lose weight and inches, gain weight and build muscle mass, or establish and maintain a high level of physical fitness needs to weight train a minimum of 2-3 days a week. On alternate days you can do generalized aerobic exercise such as fast walking, stationary biking or jogging. Initially, after a 10-15 minute warm-up, each weight training session should last no longer than one hour. After the first three months you will have given your body a chance to become accustomed to weight training and will begin to feel confident about lengthening your workouts and incorporating one or more of the eight weight training principles.

The following is a suggested routine you can perform to begin your weight training program:

BEGINNING ROUTINE

Exercise	Sets	Reps
Five to ten minutes of warm-up exercises.		
1. Crunches (abdominals)	2	20-40
2. Incline Bench Press (chest)	2-3	8-12
3. Seated Dumbbell Press (shoulders)	2-3	8-12
4. Bicep Curl (biceps)	2-3	8-10
5. Tricep Extension (triceps)	2	8-10
6. Lat Machine Pulldown (back)	2	8-12
7. Leg Extension (legs-quadriceps)	2-3	8-12
8. Leg Curl (legs-hamstrings)	3	8-12
Five to ten minutes of cool-down exercises.		

You will have to rely on your own intuition to determine what amount of weight to use. Normally, when beginning your weight training program use less weight to familiarize yourself with the exercise. Once you have learned the exercise and can perform it correctly, gradually add weight until you cannot complete the last rep with good form. If a set calls for 8-12 reps and you can perform 15 comfortably, the weight is too light. Conversely, if you cannot perform more than 7-8 reps the weight is too heavy. Using this method will ensure correct intensity. Move through your workout at a good pace.

Reps And Sets

The number of repetitions performed in one set will depend upon the muscle group being worked. The upper body muscle groups (chest, back, shoulders, upper arms) should be kept within the range of 8-12 reps per set. The legs should be kept within the range of 10-14 reps per set and abdominal exercises between 25-100 reps per set. The calves and forearms respond best to 15-20 reps per set.

The number of repetitions performed will vary between muscle groups for the following two reasons: First, some muscles have a greater content of endurance-promoting fibers (slow-twitch muscle fibers), while others have a greater content of strength-promoting fibers (fast-twitch muscle fibers). Second, muscles that are used on a regular basis during the day are composed of muscle fibers that have been toughened to exercise and require additional stimulation with increased reps and weight.

Performing 4-6 reps with a moderately heavy weight will develop greater strength and muscle mass. Performing 8-12 reps with a lighter weight will produce greater muscular endurance.

Varying Your Weight Training Program

Your body and its nervous system are very adaptable to the demands being placed on it. If you were to begin a weight training program and continue to perform the same sets with the same weights, over a period of time your body would begin to respond at an increasingly slower rate. To keep progressing in your weight training program, change your workouts on a regular basis. This can be accomplished by varying one or more of the eight weight training principles.

Resting Between Sets

The amount of time between sets will depend upon your present level of fitness. During an average weight training session you should rest approximately one minute between sets. This will give your body time to recover from the previous set and prepare for the next one. The rest interval will be shorter when working smaller muscle groups such as biceps and triceps and longer when working larger muscle groups such as legs and back. If you begin to feel faint or light-headed after a set, take an extended rest interval to regain your composure. Try reducing the number of reps or amount of weight used in the next set.

Proper Form

Proper form is important to successful weight training. Performing exercises correctly will place the maximum load on the muscle being worked. Sacrificing form for additional weight will yield poor results. Incorporating other body parts into the movement, such as jerking, or swinging a weight or body part to get moving is called cheating.

When performing an exercise it is important to maintain the recommended body position and move the body joint/muscle through its full range of motion. The muscle being worked should be allowed to move from full extension to full contraction and back to full extension during each repetition performed. Movements shorter than this will not allow the muscle to work up to its full capacity.

Breathing

There has always been a debate concerning the proper breathing technique to use when performing an exercise. In most cases, it makes no difference how you breathe as long as you breathe during the exercise. When you are unsure, the best thing to do is breathe normally. This will keep you from blacking out or experiencing a feeling of dizziness. If you must follow a breathing pattern, the one most often used is inhaling during least resistance and exhaling during maximum resistance.

Recovering From A Workout

Your muscles will grow in size and strength when allowed to fully recover following a weight training session. Recovery will take anywhere from 48-72 hours depending on how hard your muscles were worked. This recovery process will require you to rest periodically during the day and get sufficient sleep during the night. Periodic resting consists of taking a number of 15 to 30 minute rest periods, evenly spaced during the day. This will become a necessity when your weight training has increased in intensity or when you find yourself becoming overstressed.

A rest period involves lying down or reclining on a soft surface and letting go both physically and mentally. This will normally refreshen and recharge your energy level. Sleep requirements vary considerably between individuals. The norm for most people is eight hours of sleep a night. I have known some individuals who function at 100% with only four or five hours per night and some who require ten to twelve before they consider beginning their day. Let your body dictate how much sleep you need. This will allow you to rise alert, energetic, and ready to start the day.

Split Routines

During the first three months of weight training, you will workout a minimum of two non-consecutive days a week. This will give your muscles 48 hours to recover before the next workout.

The most popular method for increasing the intensity of your workouts is to split up your routine to work two or more muscle groups on a different day. This is known as a split routine.

In the basic split routine you will work three muscle groups on Monday and Thursday, and remaining muscle groups on Tuesday and Friday. The following is an example of a four-day split routine. Abs and calves are worked on alternate days.

4-Day Program

Monday – Thursday	Tuesday – Friday
Abs	Abs
Chest	Legs
Triceps	Biceps/Forearms
Shoulders	Back
Calves	Calves

If you want to intensify your workouts even further, you can choose either a five- or six-day split routine. The five-day split routine divides your workouts so you are weight training the same muscle groups on alternate days.

The following is an example of a five-day split routine. Monday's routine is always alternated.

5-Day Program

Monday – Wednesday – Friday	Tuesday – Thursday
Abs	Abs
Legs	Chest
Biceps/Forearms	Triceps
Back	Shoulders
Calves	Calves

The six-day split routine is the most intense workout program you can follow. This is normally the training schedule followed by men and women who are involved in advanced bodybuilding. The following is an example of a six-day split routine.

6-Day Program

Mon – Thurs	Tues – Fri	Wed – Sat
Abs	Abs	Abs
Chest	Triceps	Legs
Shoulders	Biceps	Back
Calves	Forearms	Calves

Advanced Weight Training

You will inevitability reach a level in your weight training where you would like to make greater gains in muscle size and strength. When this happens, there are several techniques that can be incorporated into your weight training program to improve your workouts.

After completing your warm-up, the remaining sets will be taken to the point of failure. This is when you can no longer complete a rep without additional help. There are two methods used to bring muscle to the point of failure; forced reps, and strip sets. The remaining techniques: compound sets; trisets; negative reps; and forced negatives will also increase the intensity of your weight training.

Forced Reps — Forced reps are performed with a training partner or spotter. After your muscle is taken to the point of failure, your training partner will apply minimum pressure to help you complete your rep. An example would be the bench press. Your training partner stands at the head of the bench and pulls up on the bar with enough pressure to keep it moving. Each additional rep would require your training partner to apply a little more pressure.

Strip Sets — This is a method by which weight is progressively removed from an exercise machine or barbell during the execution of an exercise. Using the bench press as an example, place two spotters at opposite ends of the bar to remove a predetermined amount of weight each time you reach the point of failure. The bar should be plate loaded with a variety of plates so you can perform 4-6 strict reps. After reaching the point of failure, without resting, have spotters remove a predetermined amount of weight from each end of the bar. Perform another set until you reach the point of failure, and again, remove more weight. If you are still going strong, repeat the process again to the point of total muscle fatigue. When finished, you will experience a "pumped" sensation you have never felt before.

Compound Sets — Compound sets will increase the inten-sity of your weight training as you will be performing two exercises, back to back, with no rest interval between sets, followed by a normal rest interval.

Trisets — Trisets are identical to compound sets except that three exercises are performed one after the other, followed by a normal rest interval. Trisets can be performed with any muscle group or combination of muscle groups.

Negative Reps — Negative reps are performed by lowering a weight at a much slower pace than was raised.

33

Forced Negatives — Forced negatives are performed with exercise machines and free weights. You will raise the weight under your own power and resist additional negative pressure being applied by your training partner or spotter. When performing pure negatives you will be able to use a weight 30-50% heavier. Your training partner will provide the neces-sary assistance to raise the weight to the starting position.

Overtraining

There are two types of overtraining: *general* and *local*. General overtraining affects the whole body producing stagnation and decreased physical performance. When local overtraining occurs only one specific body part or muscle group is affected. Local overtraining can be experienced by most persons involved in weight training and is recognized by soreness and stiffness after performing a particular exercise.

When overtraining is not acknowledged and allowed to become serious it can take weeks or even months for your body to recover. Overtraining must not be confused with exhaustion. Exhaustion is a reaction to the short-term im-balance between stress and how your body is adapting to it. Overtraining is the result of a prolonged imbalance and is a long, slow process with many obvious characteristics. The key is recognizing the warning signs and taking steps to alleviate the problem before it gets worse.

The following characteristics can be used to identify an approaching "overtrained" condition:

1. **A noticeable decrease in strength or overall performance level.**

2. **Overall fatigue.** You don't recover from previous workouts as well as you did before. You become susceptible to headaches, colds, and fever blisters.

3. **General muscle soreness.** You begin to experience a slow, general increase in muscle soreness and stiffness after a hard workout.

4. **You begin to sleep longer than normal and still feel tired.**

5. **You begin to realize a drop in body weight.** This is an easy sign to spot, especially when no effort is being made to lose weight.

6. **Your resting heart rate is higher than normal.** To check your resting heart rate take your pulse each day under the same conditions. If your resting heart rate is 10 beats higher than normal, your metabolism has not recovered from the previous workout. Keep in mind that it normally takes 90 minutes to 2 hours for your pulse rate to return to normal, even after a short workout.

7. **The recovery time between sets and workouts is longer than normal.**

8. **Your body temperature is higher than normal.** You begin to feel hot and feverish. This is an important sign that you may be reaching the point of heat exhaustion or heat stroke.

9. **You begin to lose your appetite.** This could be one of the reasons for a decrease in body weight.

10. **Your coordination becomes impaired.** You have a difficult time performing exercises with the same pace and coordination you had in previous workouts.

11. **You experience a swelling of the lymph nodes in your neck, groin, or armpits.** This, along with an increased body temperature, is a symptom requiring immediate attention.

12. **You become psychologically and emotionally drained.** This includes increased nervousness, depression, inability to relax and poor motivation .

The general cause of overtraining is weight training too hard, too soon. In other words, exceeding your body's ability to adapt to the new workload being imposed.

Your body has a limited capacity to adapt and when it is overstressed you begin to experience the symptoms of overtraining. Your body is trying to tell you to slow down and let it recover.

Saunas
And Steambaths

A great place to relax after a hard workout is in either a steambath or sauna. Sauna heat and steam will have varying effects on your body and skin. Therefore, it is necessary to understand their differences for safe use.

The air in a sauna is heated by hot, porous rocks that radiate a constant, long-lasting heat. A sauna is similar to a convection oven in that the heat is evenly distributed over your body. If you take a higher seat in a sauna you will discover the air becomes increasingly hotter. Because the overall humidity is normally 4-10%, saunas are constructed of wood.

The steambath is different from a sauna in that water vapor in the air radiates the heat. A steambath may seem considerably hotter than a sauna but it is actually several degrees cooler;

120°F for the steambath versus 170° to 180°F for the sauna. This is due to the fact that body heat is more efficiently dissipated in dry air.

When the outside air temperature rises above 98.6°F, the blood vessels in the skin begin to dilate, allowing more blood to pass through them. The heat from your blood is then transferred to the surface of the skin. As your body temperature rises, signals are transmitted from temperature sensors in your lower brain to the sweat glands in your skin. This is when you begin to sweat. The fluid that is produced is 99.1% water and is drawn from the blood to the surface of the skin. With sweat on your skin, the excess body heat can be used to evaporate the water. Thus, sweating lets your body rid itself of excess heat.

Here are several tips to consider if you are going to use a sauna or steambath.

1. Be sure to drink plenty of water or fruit juices.

2. Wait at least 30 minutes after eating.

3. Jewelry conducts heat very efficiently and can cause minor burns.

4. If your health is questionable, consult with your physician before entering a sauna or steambath.

5. If you are pregnant, a prolonged exposure to heat should be avoided. Check with your obstetrician if you intend to use a sauna or steambath. The same applies when using a whirlpool.

Using a whirlpool is not recommended if you have open cuts or wounds, as the water may promote infection.

Weight Training Myths

At some point you may have been introduced to myths concerning weight training. The following are six of the most popular:

1. **Weight training makes women unfeminine.**
   Fact: Weight training will help develop a well proportioned, firm and healthy body.

2. **Your muscle tissue will turn to fat as soon as you quit weight training.**
   Fact: It is physiologically and chemically impossible for muscle to turn into fat. Your muscles will slowly atrophy, or return to their original size.

3. **Weight training will ruin your back, knees, and joints.**
   Fact: When performed correctly, weight training will improve the overall health and strength of your back, knees, and joints.

4. **Weight training will slow you down.**
   Fact: If this were true, no one would be training with weights, especially athletes.

2
STRETCHING EXERCISES

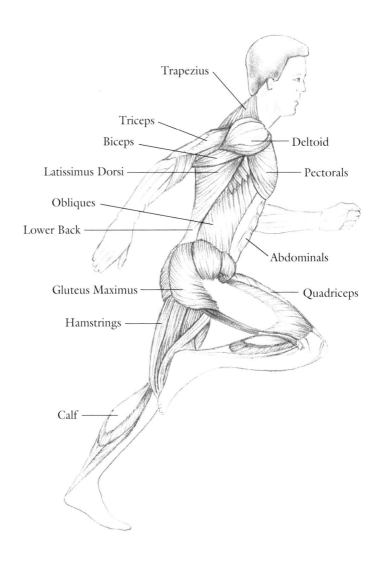

Trapezius

Triceps

Biceps

Latissimus Dorsi

Obliques

Lower Back

Gluteus Maximus

Hamstrings

Calf

Deltoid

Pectorals

Abdominals

Quadriceps

ALTERNATE TOE TOUCHES

Muscles Involved: The hamstrings and lower back.

Execution: Stand with your feet a little wider than shoulder-width apart and extend your arms straight out to the sides.

1. Bend forward and twist to the left touching your left foot with your right hand; 2. Return to the starting position; 3. Repeat to the opposite side touching your right foot with the left hand; 4. Alternate from side to side until you have performed 12-15 reps per side.

CALF STRETCHES

Muscles Involved: The calf muscles.

Execution: Stand 2 to 3 feet away from a wall and lean on it with your forearms. Bend one leg, placing your foot on the floor in front of you while keeping the other leg straight behind you. Point the toes straight ahead or turn them in slightly.

1. Slowly move your hips forward keeping the heel of the straight leg on the floor, do not bounce; 2. Hold this stretch for 30 seconds; 3. Repeat with the other leg.

FEET APART
SEATED FORWARD BENDS

Muscles Involved: The hamstrings and lower back.

Execution: Sit on the floor with your legs straight and spread wide apart.

1. Bend forward as far as possible and touch the floor in front of you; 2. Hold this position for a few seconds; 3. Move your hands over to your left leg and grasp it as far down the leg as possible, slowly pulling for a maximum stretch; 4. Hold this position for a few seconds; 5. Move your hands over to your right leg and grasp it as far down the leg as possible, slowly pulling for a maximum stretch; 6. Hold this position for a few seconds; 7. Repeat as required.

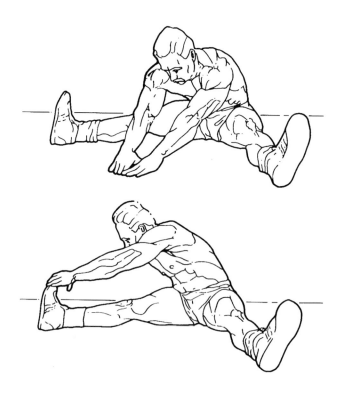

FORWARD BENDS

Muscles Involved: The hamstrings and lower back.

Execution: Stand upright with your feet together and bend forward taking hold of your ankles.

> 1. Slowly pull with your arms bringing your head as close to your legs as possible, do not bounce; 2. Hold this position for 30 to 45 seconds; 3. Slowly relax and return to the starting position; 4. Repeat as required.

Miscellaneous: If you cannot reach your ankles when bending over then grasp the back of your legs at the lowest possible point.

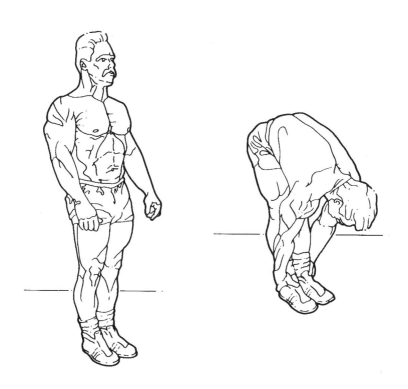

INNER THIGH STRETCHES

Muscles Involved: The inner thighs.

Execution: Sit on the floor with your knees out to the sides and the soles of your feet together.

1. Grasp your feet and slowly pull them in as close to your groin as possible; 2. Slowly relax your legs and press your knees toward the floor as far as possible, do not bounce your legs; 3. Hold this position for 30 to 45 seconds and then relax; 4. Repeat as required.

QUADRICEPS STRETCHES

Muscles Involved: The front of the thighs.

Execution: Kneel on the floor with your feet far enough apart so you can sit between them and place your hands on the floor behind you.

> 1. Slowly lean back as far as possible; 2. Hold this position for 30 to 45 seconds; 3. Slowly relax and return to the starting position; 4. Repeat as required.

Miscellaneous: If you are unable to lean back very far do not be alarmed. Your overall flexibility will improve as you continue with your weight training program.

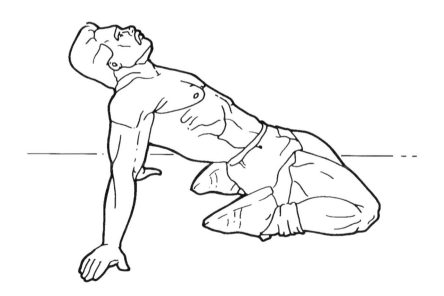

SHOULDER STRETCHES

Muscles Involved: The shoulders and back.

Execution: Stand with a towel in your hands shoulder-width apart, arms straight and resting on your upper thighs.

1. Slowly lift your arms, moving them upward and to the rear, "dislocating" your shoulders, so the towel comes to rest across the back of your thighs; 2. Reverse the movement and slowly return to the starting position; 3. Repeat as required.

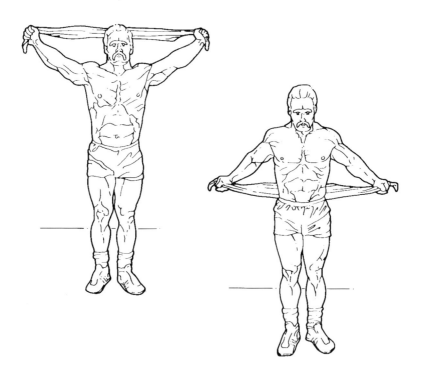

SIDE BENDS

Muscles Involved: The obliques.

Execution: Stand erect with your arms at your sides, feet shoulder-width apart.

1. Slowly bend your left side, running your left hand down your body as far as possible; 2. Slowly return to the starting position; 3. Slowly bend your right side, running your right hand as far down your body as possible; 4. Repeat as required.

Miscellaneous: When performed correctly, this exercise is relatively difficult since you rarely stretch in the lateral plane.

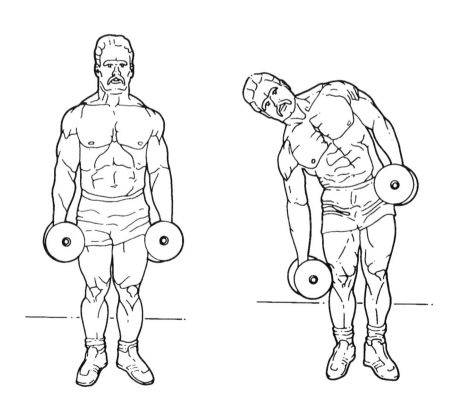

SPINAL TWISTS

Muscles Involved: The internal and external obliques.

Execution: Sit on the floor with your legs extended in front of you. Bend your right knee and twist your torso placing your left elbow on the outside of your raised knee. Place your other hand on the floor behind you for support.

1. Slowly twist to the right as far as possible; 2. Hold this position for 30 seconds; 3. Slowly relax and return to the starting position; 4. Repeat with the left leg in the opposite direction; 5. Repeat as required.

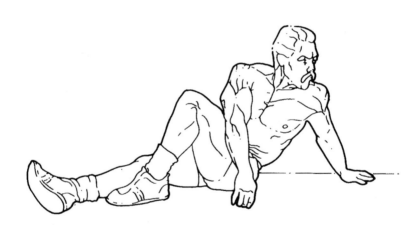

3
ABDOMINAL EXERCISES

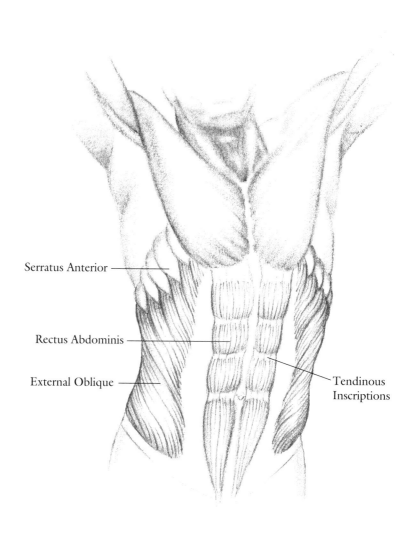

Serratus Anterior

Rectus Abdominis

External Oblique

Tendinous
Inscriptions

ALTERNATE KNEE RAISES

Muscles Involved: The rectus abdominis, external oblique and internal oblique.

Execution: Lean back on the floor supporting yourself with your hands under your buttocks and upper body resting on the elbows. Lift both legs off the floor.

1. Slowly bring your left leg up toward your shoulder as close as possible; 2. Straighten out your left leg and simultaneously bring the other knee up to your shoulder; 3. Repeat as required.

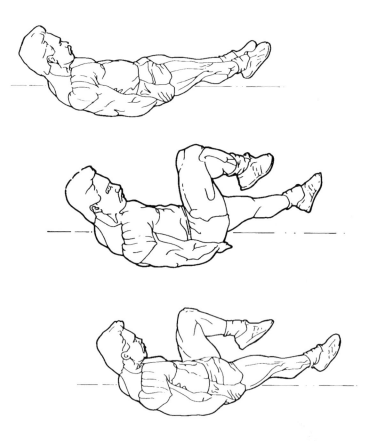

BENT-KNEE
HANGING LEG RAISES

Muscles Involved: The rectus abdominis, external oblique and internal oblique.

Execution: Grasp hold of a chinning bar with an overhand grip and hang at arm's length.

  1. Slowly bend your knees and lift your legs as high as possible;
  2. Slowly lower them back to the starting position; 3. Repeat as required.

Miscellaneous: Bent-knee hanging raises are great for concluding your ab workout when performed slowly and deliberately. Lifting wraps are recommended if you cannot maintain your grip.

BENT-KNEE
VERTICAL LEG RAISES

Muscles Involved: The rectus abdominis, external oblique and internal oblique.

Execution: Support yourself with your arms on a vertical bench with your legs fully extended.

1. Keep your upper body steady and slowly bend your knees and raise your legs up as far as possible; 2. Slowly lower your legs back to the starting position; 3. Repeat as required.

Miscellaneous: To maintain proper form, keep your lower back against the back support at all times.

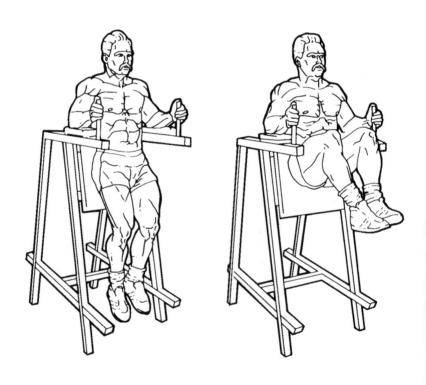

BENT-OVER TWISTS

Muscles Involved: The rectus abdominis, external oblique and internal oblique.

Execution: Place a bar across the back of your shoulders and assume a bent-over position. Your feet should be slightly wider than shoulder-width apart, your back slightly arched and knees slightly bent.

1. Slowly rotate your shoulders trying to touch the end of the bar with the opposite foot, (i.e., right tip of the barbell to left foot and left tip of barbell to right foot); 2. Keeping your back parallel to the floor, return to the starting position and repeat to the opposite side; 3. Repeat as required.

Miscellaneous: Always keep your back slightly arched. An important benefit from performing bent-over twists correctly is a stronger lower back.

CRUNCHES

Muscles Involved: The rectus abdominis, external oblique and internal oblique.

Execution: Locate a space on the floor where you will not be disturbed. Lie on your back with your legs up in the air and feet crossed. Interlace your hands behind your head or cross them at your chest.

1. Raise your head and shoulders off the floor as high as possible. You will only have a range of motion of approximately 30-45 degrees; 2. Slowly lower yourself to the starting position; 3. Repeat as required at a moderate pace.

Miscellaneous: Performing crunches with your hands behind your neck may appear easier as the range of motion is smaller. If you want a more intense abdominal workout, place your hands across your chest and touch your elbows to your knees. This method eliminates possible injury to your neck.

FLAT BENCH LEG RAISES

Muscles Involved: The rectus abdominis, external oblique and internal oblique.

Execution: Sit on the end of a flat exercise bench and grasp the end of the bench for support. Lean back and extend your legs straight out.

1. Keep your legs straight and slowly raise them as high as you can; 2. Slowly lower your legs until they are below bench level; 3. Repeat as required.

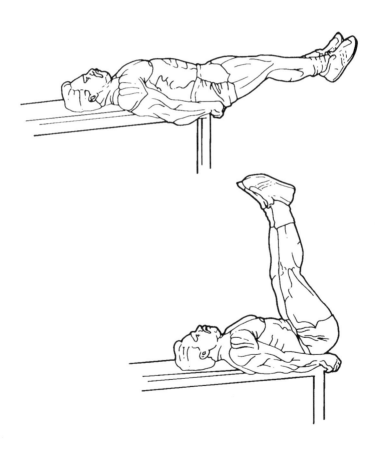

HANGING LEG RAISES

Muscles Involved: The rectus abdominis, external oblique and internal oblique.

Execution: Jump up and grasp a chinning bar with an over-hand grip and hang at arm's length from the bar.

1. Keep your legs straight and slowly raise them in front of you as far as possible; 2. Slowly lower your legs back to the starting position; 3. Repeat as required.

Miscellaneous: If this exercise is too difficult to perform, begin by using bent knees. This will decrease the overall resistance by one-half.

JACK KNIVES

Muscles Involved: The rectus abdominis, external oblique and internal oblique.

Execution: Lie on your back and extend your legs straight up.

1. Keeping your legs up and straight, slowly reach upward toward your toes with your fingers; 2. Return to the starting position; 3. Repeat as required.

Miscellaneous: If you have a difficult time performing this exercise, try propping your feet against a wall.

REVERSE TRUNK TWISTS

Muscles Involved: The rectus abdominis, external oblique and internal oblique.

Execution: Lie on your back with your arms straight out from your sides and legs extended straight up from the floor (vertical). If you experience tension in your legs, bend them slightly.

1. Keeping your feet together, slowly lower your legs to the left, touching the floor with your outside foot; 2. Slowly raise your legs back to the starting position; 3. Repeat to the opposite side; 4. Repeat as required.

Miscellaneous: To properly perform this exercise keep your shoulders and arms on the floor at all times. This will provide maximum stretching and strengthening of the internal and external obliques.

ROMAN CHAIR SIT-UPS

Muscles Involved: The rectus abdominis, external oblique and internal oblique.

Execution: Sit on the Roman Chair and place your feet under the foot support. Fold your arms across your chest.

1. Slowly lower yourself back approximately 70 degrees or until your lower back touches the chair; 2. Slowly raise back up to the starting position; 3. Repeat as required.

Miscellaneous: To place the maximum amount of stress on your abs, do not go beyond 90 degrees, or when your torso is parallel to the floor. As you reach the top of the movement, come forward as far as possible and flex and crunch your abdominal muscles to increase the contraction.

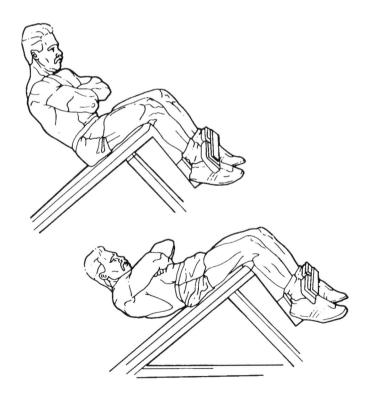

SIT-UPS

Muscles Involved: The rectus abdominis, external oblique and internal oblique.

Execution: Lie back on a sit-up board with your knees slightly flexed and feet firmly secured under the support strap or rollers. Place your hands behind your head or on your hips.

1. Slowly sit up, attempting to touch your elbows to your knees; 2. Without allowing your back to touch the board, slowly lower yourself back to the starting position; 3. Repeat as required.

Miscellaneous: Do not perform sit-ups with the legs straight as this can lead to lower back problems. As your abs become more developed the sit-up should be modified to increase the difficulty. This can be accomplished by increasing the angle of the sit-up board, placing weight on the chest, behind the head, or using a roman chair.

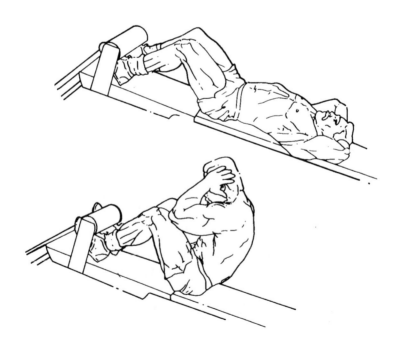

TWISTING CRUNCHES

Muscles Involved: The rectus abdominis, external oblique and internal oblique.

Execution: Lie with your back on the floor and clasp your hands behind your head. Bend your knees and raise your legs into the air crossing them at the ankles.

1. Slowly sit up, bringing your left elbow to your right knee;
2. Slowly lower yourself back to the starting position;
3. Slowly sit up, bringing your right elbow to your left knee;
4. Repeat as required.

Miscellaneous: This exercise will work a larger part of the abdominal area, including the obliques and intercostals.

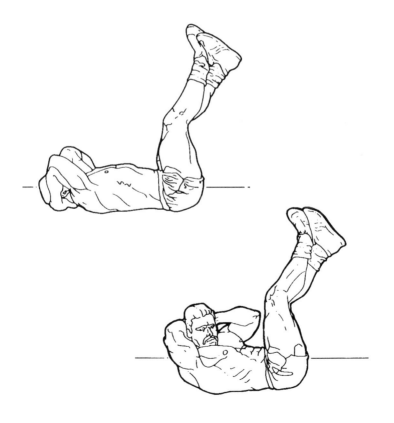

TWISTING SIT-UPS

Muscles Involved: The rectus abdominis, external oblique and internal oblique.

Execution: Lie back on a flat or incline sit-up board with your knees slightly flexed and feet firmly secured under the support strap or rollers. Clasp your hands behind your head.

1. Slowly sit up, twisting to touch your left elbow to your right knee; 2. Without allowing your back to touch the board, slowly lower yourself to the starting position; 3. Slowly sit up again, twisting to touch your right elbow to your left knee; 4. Return to the starting position; 5. Repeat as required.

Miscellaneous: Do not perform sit-ups with straight legs as this can lead to lower back problems.

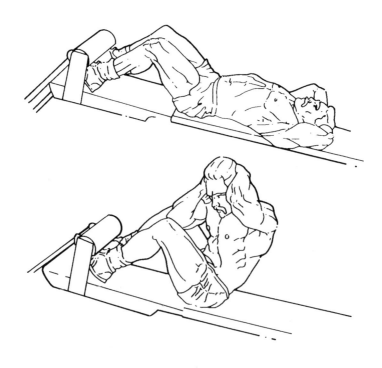

4
CHEST
EXERCISES

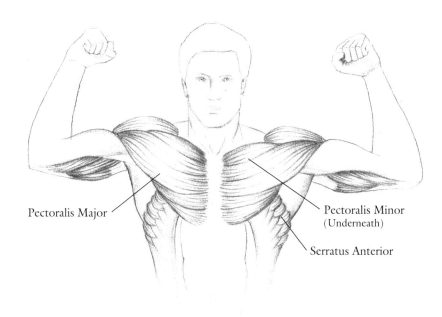

Pectoralis Major

Pectoralis Minor
(Underneath)

Serratus Anterior

BENCH PRESS

Muscles Involved: The pectorals, front deltoids, and triceps.

Execution: Lie back on the bench with your head under the barbell rack and feet flat on the floor. Grasp the barbell with an overhand grip, hands equally spaced, about shoulder-width apart.

1. Press the barbell off the rack so it is directly above your chest; 2. Slowly bend your elbows allowing the bar to descend to the middle of your chest; 3. Slowly press the barbell back to the starting position; 4. Repeat as required.

Miscellaneous: When performing this exercise with heavy weights always have a spotter. If you are unable to finish that last rep, your spotter will assist with additional encouragement.

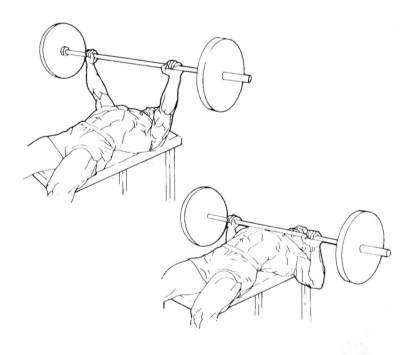

BENT-ARM PULLOVERS

Muscles Involved: The lower pectoralis major and minor, latissimus dorsi, teres major and rhomboid.

Execution: Lie with your back and shoulders across the length of the bench with your feet flat on the floor. Position your body so your upper arms will clear the bench when your arms are extended back. Grasp the dumbbell with both hands and support it directly over your chest with your hands pressing against the bottom plate, arms slightly bent.

1. Keeping your elbows in and flexed, slowly lower the dumbbell backwards in an arc over your head until your upper arms are directly in line with your body;   2. Slowly lift (pullover) the dumbbell and return to the starting position; 3. Repeat as required.

Miscellaneous: To receive maximum benefits from the pullover it must be performed with flexed elbows through the entire range of motion. To obtain a maximum stretch and expansion of the rib cage lower your hips toward the floor as you arc the dumbbell behind you.

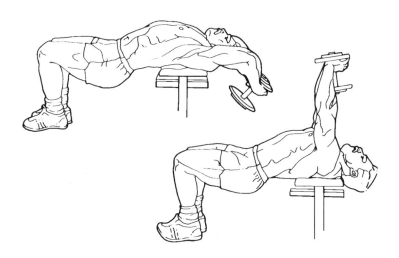

CABLE CROSSOVERS

Muscles Involved: The pectoral muscles.

Execution: Grasp the handles of an overhead pulley and assume a bent-over position with your trunk at an angle between 30-45 degrees. Keep your back slightly arched.

1. Bend your elbows slightly and pull downward and inward until your hands meet in front of you; 2. Slowly allow your arms to return to the starting position; 3. Repeat as required.

Miscellaneous: Before beginning the downward-inward pull you should feel a slight tension across your chest. To place greater stress on the upper, middle and lower pectorals, vary the height of the pulleys.

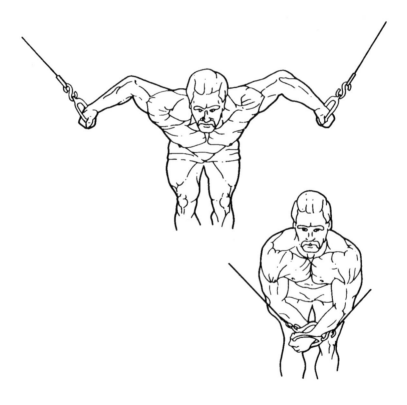

DECLINE BENCH PRESS

Muscles Involved: The lower pectoral muscles.

Execution: Lie back on the bench with your head at the lower end and knees over the edge, feet secured under the pads. In this position, grasp the bar with an evenly spaced, shoulder-width overhand grip.

1. Press the barbell off the rack so it is directly above your chest; 2. Slowly lower the barbell until it touches your lower chest; 3. Slowly press the barbell back to the starting position; 4. Repeat as required.

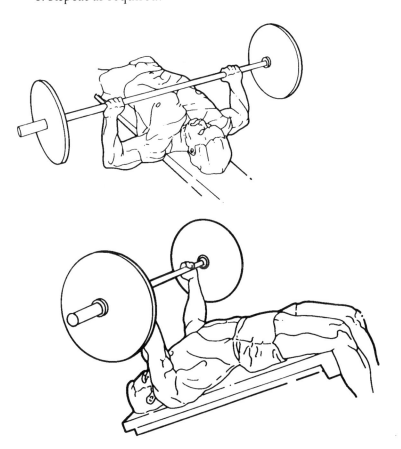

DIPS

Muscles Involved: The pectoral muscles and triceps.

Execution: If the dip bars are adjustable, position them shoulder-width or slightly wider than shoulder-width apart. Grasp the bars and jump up to support yourself with arms completely extended and elbows locked. Bend the knees slightly to avoid contact with the floor.

1. Slowly lower your body as far as possible without losing control; 2. Slowly press your body up until you return to the starting position; 3. Repeat as required.

Miscellaneous: With this exercise you can elect to go wider than shoulder-width apart. This will minimize the anterior deltoid and triceps, bringing the latissimus dorsi, lower pectoralis major and teres major into play. If you elect to go less than shoulder-width apart the triceps become heavily stressed.

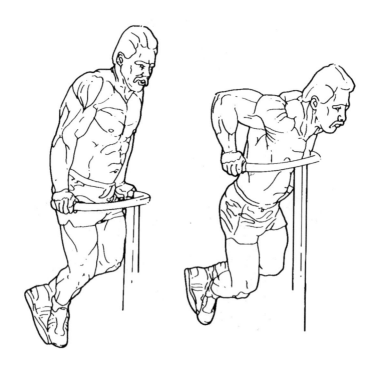

DUMBBELL BENCH PRESS

Muscles Involved: The pectorals, front deltoids, and triceps.

Execution: Take two dumbbells and lie back on a flat bench with your knees bent and feet flat on the bench. Hold the dumbbells at arm's length over your chest with palms facing forward.

1. Slowly lower the dumbbells toward your chest, maintaining balance and control; 2. Slowly press the dumbbells back to the starting position, locking your elbows; 3. Repeat as required.

Miscellaneous: Performing the dumbbell bench press will promote greater muscular balance as you are not compensating for the weaker arm as with the barbell bench press. For greater pectoralis major and anterior deltoid development, drop your elbows as far as possible.

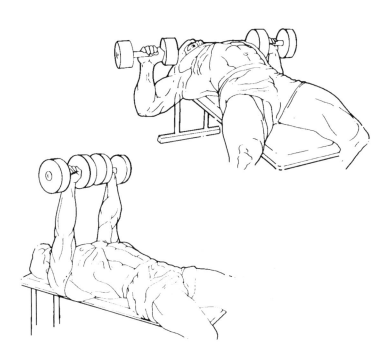

DUMBBELL FLYES

Muscles Involved: The pectoral muscles.

Execution: Grasp a dumbbell in each hand with an over-hand grip and lie back on a narrow exercise bench with your feet flat on the floor. Press the dumbbells up so the arms are fully extended and palms are facing each other.

1. Keeping the arms extended, bend slightly at the elbows and slowly move the dumbbells out to your sides in an arc to the lowest possible point; 2. Following the same arc, return the dumbbells to the starting position; 3. Repeat as required.

Miscellaneous: Do not use excessively heavy weights when performing flyes. With heavy weights you cannot perform the exercise correctly and will not achieve desired results. When performed correctly, the dumbbell flye is one of the best exercises to develop the pectoralis major muscles.

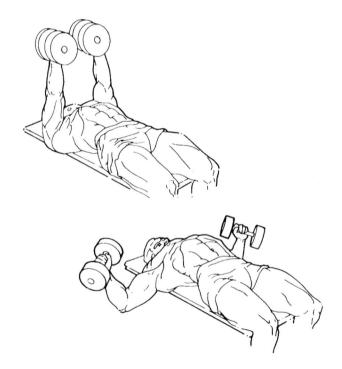

INCLINE BENCH PRESS

Muscles Involved: The upper pectorals and front deltoids.

Execution: Lie back on a 45-degree bench with your feet flat on the pedals or floor. Grasp the bar with an overhand grip, your hands spaced slightly wider than shoulder-width apart.

1. Press the barbell off the rack so it is directly above your chest with your arms fully extended and elbows locked;
2. Slowly lower the barbell until it touches your upper chest;
3. Slowly press the bar back to the starting position; 4. Repeat as required.

Miscellaneous: Initially, you may have difficulty keeping the bar in place above you. After several reps you will find the right "groove" allowing you to keep the bar from drifting. It is also recommended that you have a spotter when performing this exercise.

INCLINE DUMBBELL FLYES

Muscles Involved: The upper pectorals.

Execution: Lie back on an incline bench with your feet flat on the floor. Grasp two dumbbells with an overhand grip and hold them with your arms fully extended above your chest, palms facing each other.

1. Slowly move the dumbbells out to your sides in an arc to the lowest possible point, bending slightly at the elbows; 2. Following the same arc, return the dumbbells to the starting position; 3. Repeat as required.

Miscellaneous: To maintain proper form avoid bringing the weights in close to your body and pressing them straight up.

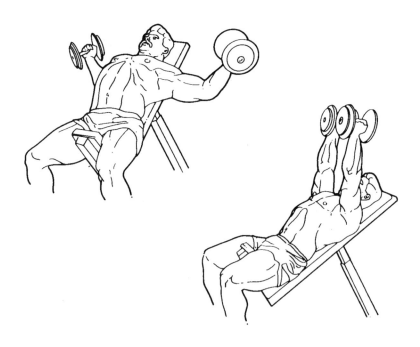

PEC DEC

Muscles Involved: The pectoral muscles.

Execution: Most clubs and gyms have an exercise machine that can approximate the flyeing movement called a pec deck. Sit into the machine and fasten the restraining belt, if provided. Place your forearms on the pads so your forearms and upper arms form a 90-degree angle.

1. Slowly squeeze your arms together until the two pads meet in front of you; 2. Slowly allow the pads to return to the starting position; 3. Repeat as required.

Miscellaneous: Using a pec deck will provide you with the fullest possible range of motion, stretching the pectorals to the maximum at full extension.

5
TRICEP
EXERCISES

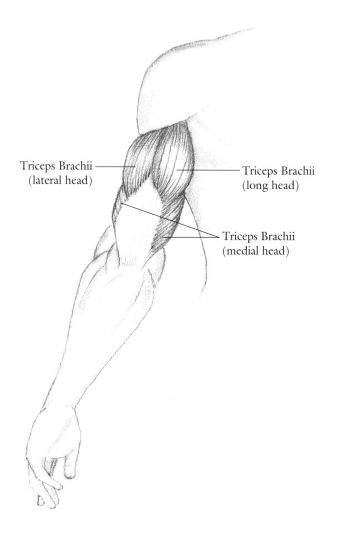

Triceps Brachii
(lateral head)

Triceps Brachii
(long head)

Triceps Brachii
(medial head)

DIPS BEHIND BACK

Muscles Involved: The triceps and pectorals.

Execution: Place two flat exercise benches parallel to each other about 3-4 feet apart. With your hands shoulder-width apart and arms fully extended, hold on to the edge of one bench and place your heels on the other.

1. Slowly bend your elbows, lowering your body as close to the floor as possible without touching it; 2. Slowly push your body back up to the starting position; 3. Repeat as required.

Miscellaneous: This exercise has also been referred to as "bench dips" or "reverse push-ups." To increase the intensity of the movement place a weight plate across your lap.

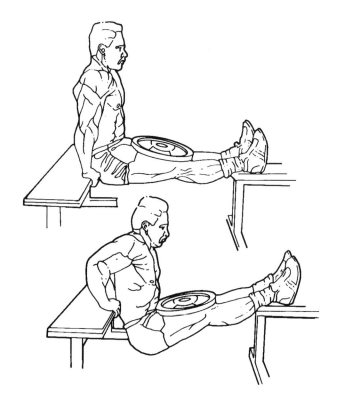

DUMBBELL KICKBACKS

Muscles Involved: The triceps brachii.

Execution: Grasp a dumbbell and assume a bent-over position with one foot in front of the other, your upper body parallel to the floor and both feet hip-width apart. Support yourself against an exercise bench with your free hand. Hold the dumbbell keeping your upper arm and elbow in line with and against your upper body with the forearm hanging straight down.

1. Keeping your upper arm in place, extend your arm to the rear until it is straight; 2. Continue this movement as far as possible after the arm is fully extended, until your hand and dumbbell are above the level of your back; 3. Slowly return the dumbbell to the starting position; 4. Repeat as required.

Miscellaneous: To keep your back in the horizontal position throughout this exercise place your free hand on a sufficiently low bench. If you cannot perform the exercise with proper form it will be necessary to reduce the amount of weight used.

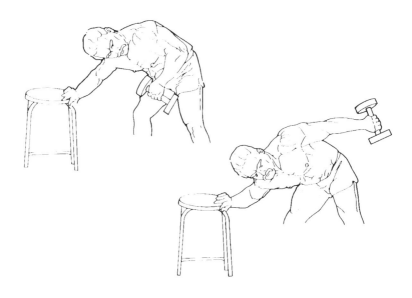

LYING CROSS FACE
TRICEPS EXTENSION

Muscles Involved: The outer triceps.

Execution: Grasp a dumbbell and lie on a flat exercise bench with your head close to the end, your knees bent and feet flat on the bench. Hold the dumbbell in your left hand at arm's length above your head.

1. Keeping your upper arm stationary, slowly lower the dumbbell across your face until it touches your right shoulder; 2. Slowly extend your arm, returning to the starting position; 3. Repeat as required, then perform the same number of reps with the opposite arm.

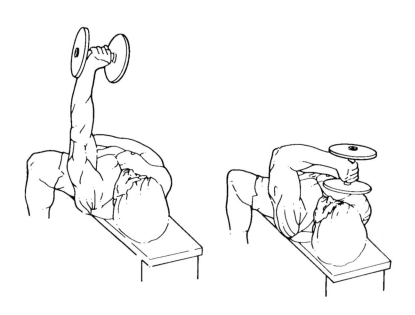

LYING TRICEPS EXTENSION

Muscles Involved: The triceps brachii.

Execution: Grasp a barbell with a narrow overhand grip (six inches or less between hands) and lay back on an exercise bench with your head at one end and feet flat on the floor. Press the bar until it is directly above your head with your palms facing toward your feet.

1. Keeping your upper arms stationary, slowly lower the barbell in a semicircle until it reaches the top of your forehead; 2. Slowly return the barbell along the same arc to the starting position; 3. Repeat as required.

Miscellaneous: To work your triceps effectively you must use a narrow grip. This will allow you to work through a greater range of motion. It is recommended that you have a spotter when performing this exercise.

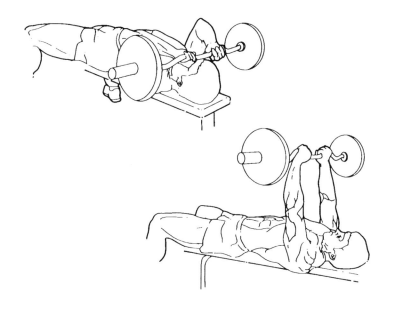

ONE-ARM
TRICEPS EXTENSION

Muscles Involved: The triceps brachii.

Execution: Grasp a dumbbell and sit on the end of a flat exercise bench, holding the dumbbell at arm's length overhead, palm facing forward. Pull your elbow in close to your head and keep your upper arm stationary.

1. Slowly lower the dumbbell in an arc behind your head (not shoulder) as far as possible; 2. Slowly extend your arm, returning the dumbbell to the starting position; 3. Repeat as required, then perform the same number of reps with the opposite arm.

Miscellaneous: To achieve maximum results, perform this movement with strict form.

SEATED TRICEPS EXTENSION

Muscles Involved: The inside and rear heads of the triceps.

Execution: Grasp a barbell with an overhand grip, hands 4-6 inches apart, and sit on the end of an exercise bench. Raise the barbell to arm's length over your head, pulling your elbows in close to your head.

1. Keeping your upper arms stationary, slowly lower the barbell in arc behind your head as far as possible; 2. Slowly press the barbell back to the starting position; 3. Repeat as required.

Miscellaneous: This exercise can be performed using a straight bar or E-Z curl bar on an incline or decline bench. Triceps extensions can also be performed in a standing position.

TRICEP PUSHDOWNS

Muscles Involved: The inside and rear heads of the triceps.

Execution: Stand close to an overhead pulley cable and grasp the bar with an overhand grip, hands 6-10 inches apart. Pull your elbows in close to your body and keep your body erect.

1. Slowly press the bar down as far as possible, locking your elbows; 2. Slowly return the bar to the middle of your chest; 3. Repeat as required.

Miscellaneous: This exercise can be performed using a variety of techniques. For example, you can vary your grip, type of bar used, width between your hands and distance of the movement.

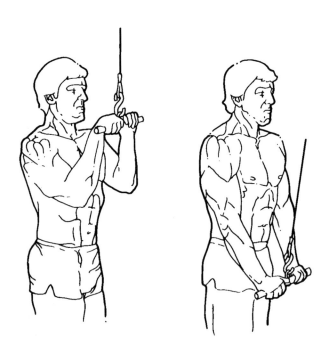

6
BICEP
EXERCISES

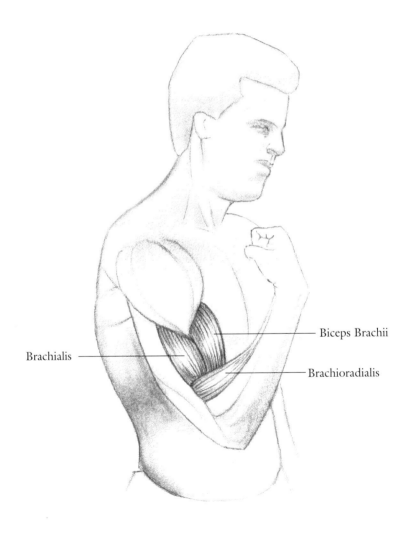

Biceps Brachii

Brachialis

Brachioradialis

ALTERNATE DUMBBELL CURLS

Muscles Involved: The biceps brachii, brachialis and brachioradialis.

Execution: Stand upright holding a dumbbell in each hand, your arms hanging fully extended, palms facing your body.

1. Slowly curl the left dumbbell up as far as possible while twisting your palm inward; 2. Slowly lower the dumbbell to the starting position; 3. Repeat with the opposite arm; 4. Repeat as required, alternating arms.

Miscellaneous: The dumbbell curl can also be performed in a seated, kneeling, and lying position.

BICEPS MACHINE CURLS

Muscles Involved: The biceps brachii, brachialis and brachioradialis.

Execution: There are several bicep machines available that operate on the same principle of stressing the bicep through the full range of motion. Adjust the seat so your shoulders are slightly below the elbows when placed on the pad. Set the weight to be used and reach over to grasp the handles with your palms up. Sit into the machine placing your elbows on the pad. Allow your arms to straighten out completely.

1. Keeping your elbows on the pad at all times, slowly curl the handles up toward the base of your neck; 2. Slowly allow the handles to return to the starting position with the arms fully extended; 3. Repeat as required.

Miscellaneous: Bicep machine curls are popular because they offer continuous resistance throughout a full range of motion. When curling with free weights, maximum resistance is experienced during the middle third of the movement. Some bicep machines will allow you to alternate arms and vary the type of resistance used.

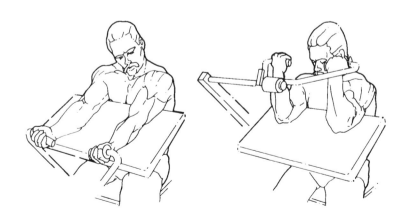

CONCENTRATION CURLS

Muscles Involved: The biceps brachii, brachialis and brachioradialis.

Execution: Grasp a dumbbell and bend over slightly allowing the dumbbell to hang at arm's length. Place your free hand on your knee or stationary object for support.

1. Slowly curl the dumbbell up to your shoulder; 2. Slowly lower the dumbbell to the starting position; 3. Repeat as required, then perform the same number of reps with the opposite arm.

Miscellaneous: As you reach your shoulder, twist the dumbbell so your thumb is lower than your little finger.

HAMMER CURLS

Muscles Involved: The biceps brachii, brachialis and brachioradialis.

Execution: Grasp two dumbbells and sit on the end of a flat exercise bench. Hold the dumbbells with palms facing together keeping your upper arms stationary.

1. Slowly curl the dumbbells up until their ends touch your shoulders; 2. Slowly lower the dumbbells back to the starting position; 3. Repeat as required.

Miscellaneous: Performing this movement will work the forearms along with the biceps.

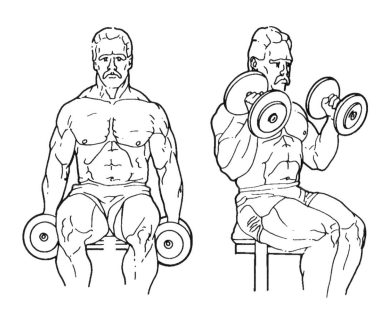

INCLINE DUMBBELL CURLS

Muscles Involved: The biceps brachii, brachialis and brachioradialis.

Execution: Grasp a dumbbell in each hand and lie back on an incline bench with your head and upper body in full contact with the pad. Your arms will hang fully extended from your sides, palms facing your body.

1. Slowly curl the dumbbells up to your shoulders keeping the elbows pointed straight down; 2. Slowly lower the dumbbells to the starting position; 3. Repeat as required.

Miscellaneous: For full involvement of the biceps, turn the weight outward so your palms face up and back when they reach your shoulders.

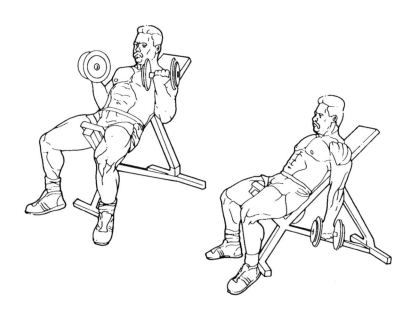

PREACHER CURLS

Muscles Involved: The biceps brachii, brachialis and brachioradialis.

Execution: Lean over the preacher curl bench and grasp the barbell with an underhand grip, hands evenly spaced, shoulder-width apart. Sit into the bench wedging your armpits over the top of the pad and run your upper arms down the surface of the bench. Allow your arms to straighten out completely.

   1. Slowly curl the barbell up until it reaches the base of your throat; 2. Slowly lower the barbell until it reaches the starting position or until the arms are fully extended; 3. Repeat as required.

Miscellaneous: To vary the intensity of this exercise change your grip from very narrow to as wide as the bar permits. This movement can be performed with an E-Z curl bar or with dumb-bells.

PULLEY CURLS

Muscles Involved: The biceps brachii, brachialis and brachioradialis.

Execution: Attach a curl bar to the cable running through a floor pulley and grasp the bar with a narrow underhand grip. Stand back from the floor pulley with your feet shoulder-width apart, arms straight and upper arms tight against the body.

1. Slowly curl the bar from the starting position until it reaches a point just under the chin; 2. Slowly allow the bar to return to the starting position; 3. Repeat as required.

Miscellaneous: This exercise can also be performed one arm at a time with a loop handle attached to the pulley cable.

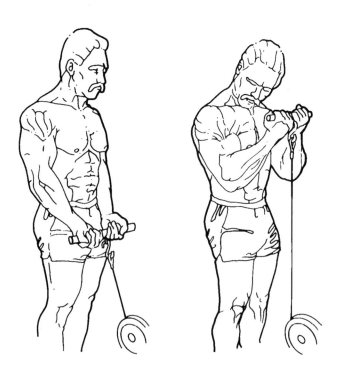

REVERSE BICEPS CURLS

Muscles Involved: The biceps brachii, brachialis and brachioradalis.

Execution: Grasp a barbell with an over-hand grip and assume a standing position with your feet and hands shoulder-width apart. Allow the barbell to rest against your thighs with your elbows touching the sides of your body.

1. Slowly curl the barbell in a semicircle to the top of your chest; 2. Slowly lower the barbell along the same arc to the starting position; 3. Repeat as required.

Miscellaneous: To place greater stress on the biceps use a narrower grip. Because of increased difficulty with a narrower grip, less weight will be required. To isolate your forearms and increase the intensity of this movement, perform it on a preacher curl bench.

SEATED DUMBBELL CURLS

Muscles Involved: The biceps brachii, brachialis and brachioradialis.

Execution: Grasp two dumbbells and sit on the end of a flat exercise bench. Hold the dumbbells with palms facing together keeping your upper arms stationary.

1. Slowly curl the dumbbells up, twisting your palms forward, to the highest possible point; 2. Slowly lower the dumbbells back to the starting position; 3. Repeat as required.

Miscellaneous: Performing this movement standing rather than seated will allow the use of more weight but your form will not be as strict. This exercise can also be performed in the same manner using a barbell

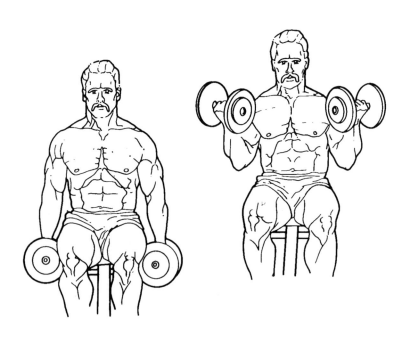

7

FOREARM
EXERCISES

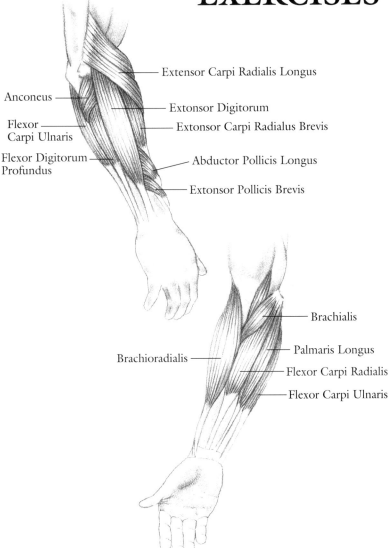

Extensor Carpi Radialis Longus

Anconeus

Extonsor Digitorum

Flexor
Carpi Ulnaris

Extonsor Carpi Radialus Brevis

Flexor Digitorum
Profundus

Abductor Pollicis Longus

Extonsor Pollicis Brevis

Brachialis

Palmaris Longus

Brachioradialis

Flexor Carpi Radialis

Flexor Carpi Ulnaris

BARBELL WRIST CURLS

Muscles Involved: The flexor carpi radials and flexor carpiularis.

Execution: Grasp a barbell with an underhand grip, hands close together, and straddle an exercise bench resting your forearms on the leading edge. Keep your elbows and wrists the same distance apart.

1. Slowly relax your wrists, lowering the bar as far as possible, while opening your fingers to increase the range of motion; 2. Slowly return the bar to the starting position; 3. Repeat as required.

Miscellaneous: To keep your elbows in tight, lock your knees in against them. Your forearm muscles are similar to your calves and abs in that they require a lot of stimulation to increase in strength and size.

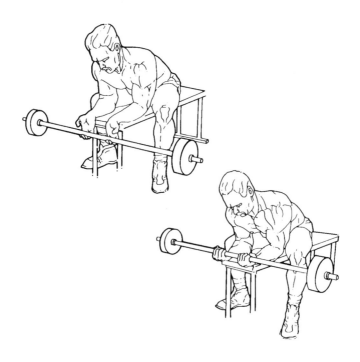

BEHIND-THE-BACK WRIST CURLS

Muscles Involved: The flexor carpi radials and flexor carpiularis.

Execution: Have someone hand you a weighted barbell from behind and hold it at arm's length, hands shoulder-width apart, palms facing toward the rear.

1. Keeping your arms flexed, slowly open your fingers and allow the bar to roll down your palms; 2. Slowly curl the bar back to the starting position; 3. Repeat as required.

DUMBBELL
ONE-ARM WRIST CURLS

Muscles Involved: The flexor carpi radials and flexor carpiularis.

Execution: Grasp a dumbbell and sit on the end of an exercise bench. Lean forward placing your forearm on your thigh, so your wrist and dumbbell are clear of your knee. Stabilize your elbow with your free hand.

1. Relax your wrist, slowly lowering the dumbbell as far as possible toward the floor, while opening your fingers slightly to increase the range of motion;   2. Slowly curl the dumbbell back to the starting position; 3. Repeat as required, then perform the same number of reps with the other arm.

REVERSE WRIST CURLS

Muscles Involved: The extensor carpi radialis longus, extensor carpi brevis and extensor carpi ulnaris.

Execution: Kneel in front of and place your forearms across an exercise bench so your hands extend beyond the far side. Your hands should be able to move through a full range of motion. Grasp the barbell or dumbbell with an overhand grip, palms facing down, and lower your hands as far as possible.

1. Slowly raise your hand(s) as high as possible or until they are perpendicular with the forearms; 2. Slowly lower to the starting position; 3. Repeat as required.

Miscellaneous: The amount of weight used will regulate your range of motion. This exercise can also be performed with dumbbells.

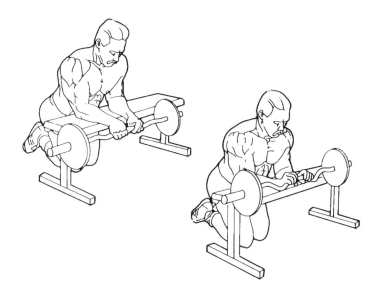

WRIST CURLS

Muscles Involved: The flexor carpi radials and flexor carpiularis.

Execution: Grasp a barbell with your hands evenly spaced 4-6 inches apart and palms facing up. Kneel in front of an exercise bench placing your forearms across the bench so your wrists extend beyond it.

1. Slowly flex your wrist joints and raise the bar up as high as possible;   2. Slowly lower the bar to the starting position; 3. Repeat as required.

Miscellaneous: The full range of motion for wrist curls is approximately 130-160 degrees, 65-80 degrees above and below the horizontal position.   If you are unable to work through this range of motion you are probably using too much weight.

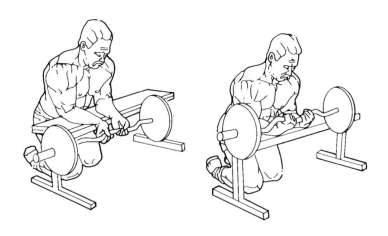

8
BACK
EXERCISES

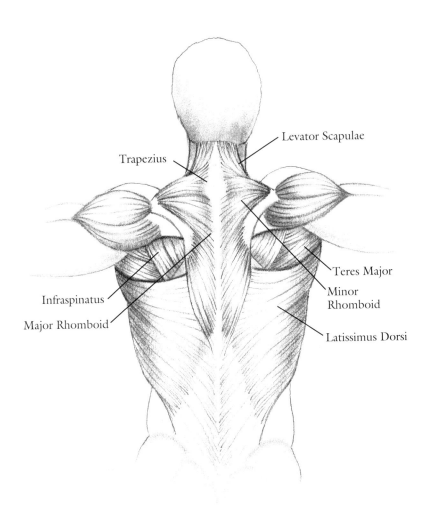

Levator Scapulae

Trapezius

Teres Major

Minor
Rhomboid

Infraspinatus

Major Rhomboid

Latissimus Dorsi

BARBELL BENT-OVER ROWS

Muscles Involved: The middle and posterior deltoid, teres minor, trapezius and rhomboid.

Execution: Stand with your feet a few inches apart and grasp a barbell with a wide overhand grip. With your knees bent slightly, bend over at the waist until your upper body is parallel with the floor. Keep your back straight and allow the barbell to hang at arm's length.

1. Slowly lift the barbell up until it touches your abs; 2. Slowly lower it back to the starting position; 3. Repeat as required.

Miscellaneous: To ensure proper development of the lats always keep your back parallel to the floor and pull the barbell up as far as your abs. Otherwise, you will be including the lower back and arms in the movement.

BENT-OVER DUMBBELL ROWS

Muscles Involved: The middle and posterior deltoid, and middle portion of the trapezius.

Execution: Grasp a dumbbell with an overhand grip and assume a bent-over position beside an exercise bench, feet shoulder-width apart. Place your free hand on the exercise bench for support, keeping your back flat and legs slightly bent.

1. Keeping the weight beside you, slowly pull up until your elbow is above your back; 2. Slowly return to the starting position; 3. Repeat as required, then perform the same number of reps with the other arm.

Miscellaneous: To maintain proper form it is important to keep your upper body stationary when performing this exercise. You will be able to use more weight in a supported position.

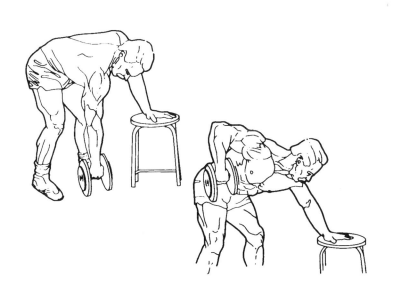

101

DUMBBELL SHRUGS

Muscles Involved: The trapezius muscles.

Execution: Stand erect with a heavy dumbbell in each hand. Keep your head stationary and chin down by focusing on a particular spot or object in front of you.

1. Keep your arms straight and slowly raise your shoulders up, as if trying to touch your ears; 2. Hold for a moment, then slowly lower your shoulders to the starting position or lowest possible point; 3. Repeat as required.

Miscellaneous: Do not pull with the arms. This movement is to be performed entirely by the trapezius muscles. It is important to keep your head firmly in place during the movement; if it isn't you will not be able to properly raise your shoulders. You can vary the movement of this exercise by rotating your shoulders to the front or back as far as possible.

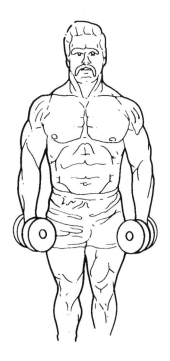 

GOOD MORNINGS

Muscles Involved: The lower back.

Execution: Grasp a barbell and place it across your shoulders. Stand with your feet a few inches apart keeping your legs and back straight.

1. Slowly bend forward at the waist, keeping your head up, until your upper body is parallel with the floor; 2. Slowly return to the starting position; 3. Repeat as required.

HYPEREXTENSIONS

Muscles Involved: The lower back.

Execution: Adjust the rear post so your feet are secured in the rear pads and your pelvis rests comfortably on the seat. Relax your upper body and allow it to hang over the seat.

1. Slowly raise your upper body until it is in line with your lower half or slightly higher; 2. Slowly relax allowing your upper body to return to the starting position; 3. Repeat as required.

Miscellaneous: Before beginning the extension try to round your spine as much as possible. This will stretch the muscles, providing more effective muscle and strength development.

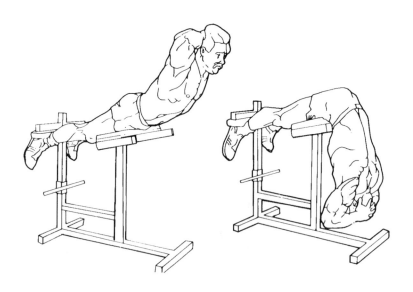

LAT PULLDOWN TO CHEST

Muscles Involved: The middle and posterior deltoid, teres minor, trapezius and rhomboid.

Execution: Grasp the bar of a lat pulldown station with a wide overhand grip. With your hands equally spaced, sit placing your legs under the padded braces.

1. Slowly pull the bar down until it touches the top of your chest; 2. Slowly return the bar to the starting position; 3. Repeat as required.

Miscellaneous: Maintaining strict form will ensure greater back development. Do not sway back when pulling the bar down as this will bring the lower back into the movement. For variation, perform the lat pulldown to the back of your neck.

NARROW GRIP LAT PULLDOWN

Muscles Involved: The middle and posterior deltoid, teres minor, trapezius and rhomboid.

Execution: Kneel or sit under the bar of a lat pulldown machine and grasp the bar with shoulder-width or narrower grip, your palms facing toward you. Your arms should be fully extended and in line with your midsection.

1. Slowly pull the bar down to your chest concentrating on bringing your elbows down in front; 2. Slowly allow the bar to return to the starting position; 3. Repeat as required.

Miscellaneous: To properly involve the major muscles, your elbows must remain in front of your body and travel in a straight downward-forward direction. If you are using weights close to your body weight, you may find it necessary to have someone assist you.

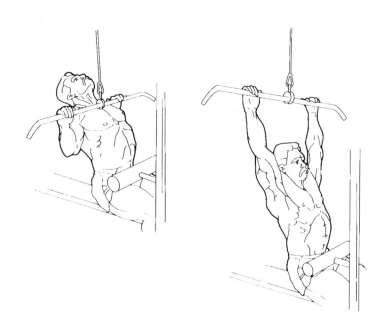

SEATED PULLEY ROWING

Muscles Involved: The middle and posterior deltoid and trapezius.

Execution: Sit down at a low cable pulley with your feet braced at the foot bar or metal plate so that your body will remain in place. Grasp the bar handle or separate pulley handles with a palms-down grip. Your trunk should be perpendicular to the floor and arms outstretched making the cable taut.

1. Pull toward your chest keeping the elbows moving back and to the sides as far as possible; 2. Slowly allow your arms to return to the starting position; 3. Repeat as required.

Miscellaneous: Your back must remain stationary throughout this exercise to ensure proper technique and correct muscle involvement. When using pulley handles, it is important to use a pronated (palms-down) grip.

STRAIGHT-ARM PULLOVER

Muscles Involved: The latissimus dorsi and pectoral muscles.

Execution: Lie on an exercise bench with your head slightly over the end and feet on the floor. Hold a barbell directly above your upper chest with your arms straight and elbows locked.

1. From this position slowly lower the barbell backwards and down until your arms are parallel with the floor; 2. Slowly begin to lift (pullover) the barbell keeping the arms straight until you reach the starting position; 3. Repeat as required.

Miscellaneous: To obtain maximum benefit from this movement, it must be performed with straight arms through the full range of motion.

T-BAR BENT-OVER ROWS

Muscles Involved: The middle and posterior deltoid, teres minor, trapezius and rhomboid.

Execution: Assume a bent-over position keeping your trunk straight and firm, placing your feet shoulder width apart with knees slightly bent. Grasp the T-bar handles with an overhand grip.

1. Pull the T-bar up to your chest keeping your elbows out to the sides and upper arms perpendicular to your trunk (your back should remain straight throughout the pull and return); 2. Slowly lower the barbell to the starting position; 3. Repeat as required.

Miscellaneous: Keep your elbows out to your sides, approximately 45 degrees, as you perform the exercise. Your back must remain stationary in the bent-over rowing position to ensure correct muscle involvement and technique.

UPRIGHT ROWS

Muscles Involved: The trapezius and front deltoids.

Execution: Stand erect and grasp a barbell with an over-hand grip, your hands 2-3 inches apart. Allow the bar to hang straight down in front of you.

1. Keeping your back straight, slowly lift the barbell up, keeping it close to your body, until it reaches your chin;
2. Slowly lower the bar back to the starting position;
3. Repeat as required.

Miscellaneous: To achieve maximum results, perform this exercise with strict form by not swinging the weight or body. This exercise can also be performed with a short bar or low pulley using the same technique. Lifting wraps are helpful if you have a difficult time maintaining your grip.

WIDE-GRIP CHINS

Muscles Involved: The middle and posterior deltoid, teres minor, trapezius and rhomboid.

Execution: Jump up and grasp a chinning bar with an over-hand grip, hands as wide as possible. Hang from the bar with your knees bent and ankles crossed to prevent touching the floor.

1. Slowly pull yourself up until the bar touches the back of your neck; 2. Slowly lower yourself back to the starting position; 3. Repeat as required.

Miscellaneous: Performing wide grip chins for the first time will normally be difficult thus limiting the number of reps. If you have a training partner, have him or her help you with a few forced reps when you can no longer complete your set. For a greater range of motion, pull up so the bar touches your upper chest rather than the back of your neck.

9
SHOULDER EXERCISES

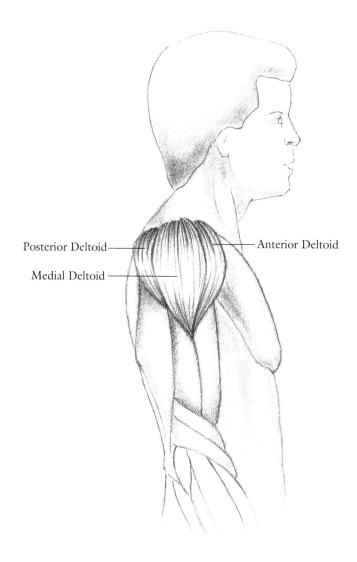

Posterior Deltoid

Anterior Deltoid

Medial Deltoid

ARNOLD PRESS

Muscles Involved: The front head of the deltoids.

Execution: Stand erect with a dumbbell in each hand. Raise the dumbbells to shoulder height with your palms facing toward you.

1. Slowly and simultaneously, press both dumbbells overhead and rotate your hands turning your palms away from your body; 2. Hold for a moment and slowly lower the dumbbells, turning your hands back to the starting position; 3. Repeat as required.

Miscellaneous: When learning this exercise be sure to go slow and easy as the turning of the dumbbells may cause you to lose control.

BEHIND-THE-NECK PRESS

Muscles Involved: The front and side deltoids.

Execution: Sit into a smith press or shoulder press bench and grasp the bar with an overhand grip, hands slightly more than shoulder-width apart. Bring the bar to shoulder level behind your neck, keeping the elbows to the outside and upper arms perpendicular to the body.

1. Slowly press the bar up until your elbows lock; 2. Slowly lower the bar back to the starting position; 3. Repeat as required.

Miscellaneous: This movement can also be performed with a barbell using the same technique. Performing this movement in a seated position will increase the strictness and intensity of the movement.

BENT-OVER CABLE LATERALS

Muscles Involved: The rear head of the deltoids.

Execution: Grasp the low cable pulley handles, left hand holding the right handle and right hand holding the left handle. With your arms crossed in front of your body, keep your back straight and bend over at the hips until your upper body is parallel with the floor.

1. Slowly pull the handles across your body and extend them out to your sides; 2. Slowly return to the starting position; 3. Repeat as required.

Miscellaneous: This exercise will provide a greater range of motion, with continuous resistance, throughout the movement.

DUMBBELL PRESS

Muscles Involved: The front deltoids.

Execution: Grasp two dumbbells and sit on the end of an exercise bench. Hold the dumbbells at shoulder height with arms bent at a 90 degree angle and palms facing forward.

1. Keeping your back straight, slowly press both dumbbells overhead until they touch at the top; 2. Slowly lower the dumbbells to the starting position; 3. Repeat as required.

Miscellaneous: The use of dumbbells will allow you to both raise and lower them through a greater range of motion. Less weight will be used as each arm is lifting independently of the other.

FRONT RAISES

Muscles Involved: The front deltoids.

Execution: Stand erect with your feet shoulder- width apart and toes pointed slightly to the sides. Grasp two dumbbells with an overhand grip. Relax your arms allowing the dumbbells to rest across your upper thighs.

> 1. Keeping your arms straight, slowly raise the left dumbbell up and forward until it is above shoulder level; 2. Hold this position for a moment; 3. Slowly lower the dumbbell back to the starting position; 4. Repeat with the opposite arm; 5. Repeat as required.

Miscellaneous: It is not necessary to use heavy weights when performing this exercise as the long lever created by straight arms will produce a greater workload. Performing this exercise in a seated position will provide a stricter movement. This exercise can also be performed with a barbell.

ONE-ARM
CROSS CABLE LATERALS

Muscles Involved: The outside and rear head of the deltoids.

Execution: Grasp the handle of a low pulley and stand erect with your arm down and across your lower body. Place your free hand on your hip.

1. Slowly pull outward and upward until your hand is slightly higher than your shoulder;   2. Slowly lower your arm to the starting position without allowing the weight plates to touch; 3. Repeat as required, then perform the same number of reps with the opposite arm.

Miscellaneous: This exercise can also be performed with the cable running behind your back. This will develop additional separation between your deltoids and upper arm.

OVERHEAD/MILITARY PRESS

Muscles Involved: The front and middle deltoid.

Execution: Sit into a smith press and grasp the bar with an overhand grip, hands slightly more than shoulder-width apart. Bring the bar to shoulder level in front of you, keeping the elbows to the outside and upper arms perpendicular to the body.

1. Slowly press the bar up until your elbows lock; 2. Slowly lower the bar back to the starting position; 3. Repeat as required.

Miscellaneous: This movement can also be performed with a barbell using the same technique. Performing the overhead press in a seated position will increase the strictness and intensity of the movement.

PRONE LATERAL RAISES

Muscles Involved: The middle and posterior deltoid.

Execution: With a dumbbell in each hand, lie face-down on a narrow exercise bench with your feet firmly planted on the floor, legs slightly bent. Hold the dumbbells with palms facing inward.

1. Keeping the elbows slightly bent, raise your arms sideways to slightly higher than shoulder height; 2. Slowly allow the dumbbells to return to the starting position; 3. Repeat as required.

Miscellaneous: This is one of the best exercises for posterior deltoid development. The major element in the performance of this exercise is the height of the elbow. The higher the elbow, the greater the muscle is worked.

121

SEATED BENT-OVER LATERALS

Muscles Involved: The rear head of the deltoids.

Execution: Grasp two dumbbells with an overhand grip and sit on the end of an exercise bench with your knees together. Bend forward at the waist and bring the dumbbells together behind your calves, palms facing together.

1. Slowly lift the dumbbells out to the sides to a point slightly higher than your back; 2. Slowly lower the dumbbells back to the starting position behind your calves; 3. Repeat as required.

Miscellaneous: Be sure to lift the dumbbells straight out to the sides. To increase the intensity of the exercise, resist and slow down the movement as you return to the starting position.

SIDE LATERAL RAISES

Muscles Involved: The outside and rear head of the deltoid.

Execution: Hold a dumbbell in each hand, palms facing toward your body, and stand erect with your feet shoulder width apart, toes pointed to the sides.

1. Bending your elbow slightly, slowly raise the dumbbell in your left hand up and to the side to slightly above shoulder level; 2. Slowly lower the dumbbell to the starting position; 3. Repeat with the other arm; 4. Repeat as required.

Miscellaneous: This exercise should be performed with strict form and light weight. Side lateral raises can also be performed in a seated position to avoid cheating.

10
LEG
EXERCISES

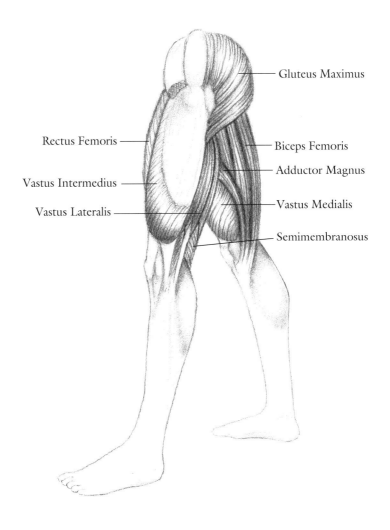

Gluteus Maximus

Rectus Femoris

Biceps Femoris

Adductor Magnus

Vastus Intermedius

Vastus Lateralis

Vastus Medialis

Semimembranosus

DEADLIFTS

Muscles Involved: The vastus lateralis, vastus medialis, vastus intermedius, rectus femoria, gluteus maximus and upper hamstrings.

Execution: Assume a position standing next to a barbell on the floor. Bend over at the hips and knees until your pelvic girdle is approximately knee level. In this position, your back should be straight and at a 45-degree angle to the floor. Keeping your arms straight, grasp the bar with a slightly wider than shoulder-width overhand grip.

1. Slowly raise your body by extending your knees and hips until you are fully erect (there should be a slight arch in your back); 2. Slowly lower the barbell back to the floor; 3. Repeat as required.

Miscellaneous: If you experience difficulty keeping your grip, try using a mixed grip (underhand/overhand). To ensure all-around development, vary the position of your feet. For example, perform the exercise with narrow, regular, and wide stances.

FRONT SQUATS

Muscles Involved: The vastus lateralis, vastus medialis, vastus intermedius, and rectus femoris.

Execution: Assume a standing position with your feet shoulder-width apart and turned slightly to the sides. Grasp the bar with your hands slightly wider than shoulder width and your elbows up high. The full weight of the bar will rest across your shoulders and upper chest. Your head should be erect or slightly tilted upward.

1. Keep your elbows up and your trunk upright and slowly lower yourself until your thighs are parallel to the floor or slightly below; 2. From this position, slowly push yourself up to the starting position; 3. Repeat as required.

Miscellaneous: During the up and down movement, keep your weight equally distributed on both feet and do not bounce or stop in the bottom position. The front squat is more difficult than the squat because of position and balancing. You will find it necessary to use less weight than the squat, especially when first performing this exercise. Remember to always keep your head and elbows up.

HACK SQUATS

Muscles Involved: The vastus lateralis, vastus medialis, vastus intermedius, rectus femoris.

Execution: Position yourself into the hack squat machine and grasp the handles or hook your shoulders under the padded bars. Place your feet together, toes pointed slightly out.

1. Press the mechanism up until your legs are fully extended;
2. Bend your knees and slowly lower yourself as far as possible;
3. Repeat as required.

Miscellaneous: This movement can be varied by changing the position of your feet. For example, place your feet at different widths and point your toes in or out.

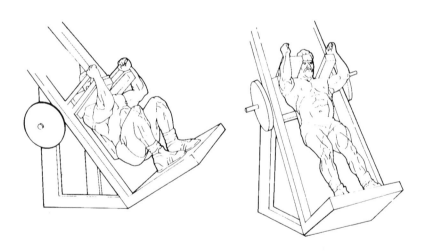

LEG ABDUCTIONS

Muscles Involved: The outer thighs and hip muscles.

Execution: Sit into a leg abduction machine and place your legs between the two padded arms. Your knees and ankles should rest comfortably against the pads. Reach down to your sides and grasp the two handles for support.

1. Slowly push your legs apart as far as possible; 2. Slowly return your legs to the starting position without allowing the weight plates to touch; 3. Repeat as required.

Miscellaneous: Several leg abductor machines have a seatbelt which will keep your torso in place during the movement.

LEG ADDUCTIONS

Muscles Involved: The inner thighs.

Execution: Sit into the leg adduction machine and spread your legs placing your knees and ankles behind the pads. Grasp the handles at your sides for support.

1. Slowly squeeze your legs together until your feet touch in front of you; 2. Slowly return your legs to the starting position without allowing the weight plates to touch; 3. Repeat as required.

Miscellaneous: Several leg adductor machines have a seatbelt which will keep your torso in place during the movement.

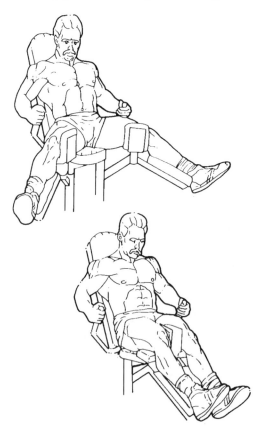

LEG CURLS

Muscles Involved: The biceps femoris, semitendinosus, and semimembranosus.

Execution: Position yourself on your stomach with your legs fully extended and knees slightly over the end of the pad. Place your heels under the roller pads and grasp the handles along side the machine to stabilize your upper body.

1. Keeping your hips on the bench, slowly curl your heels to your buttocks; 2. Slowly lower your heels back to the legs extended position; 3. Repeat as required.

Miscellaneous: You can vary the muscle worked by pointing your toes straight or drawing them toward your shins. When pointed, they allow the hamstrings to do all the work. When drawn toward your shins, the calf muscles become involved as secondary movers. This method will provide additional calf development.

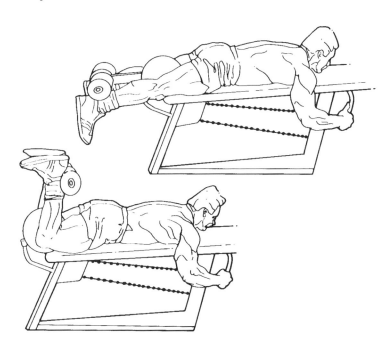

LEG EXTENSIONS

Muscles Involved: The vastus lateralis, vastus medalis, vastus intermedius, and rectus femoris.

Execution: Sit on the leg extension machine so your knees are comfortably at the end of the seat. Place your ankles behind and against the bottom rollers. If the machine has handles on the sides, grasp them. If it does not have handles, then lean back and support yourself holding onto the sides of the bench.

1. Slowly push against the bottom roller with your feet to fully extend your legs until your knee joints are completely extended; 2. Slowly allow your legs to return to the starting position without allowing the weight plates to touch; 3. Repeat as required.

Miscellaneous: It is important to lock your knees out for maximum contraction of the muscles. You also have the option of performing single leg extensions by selecting a lighter weight and alternating legs.

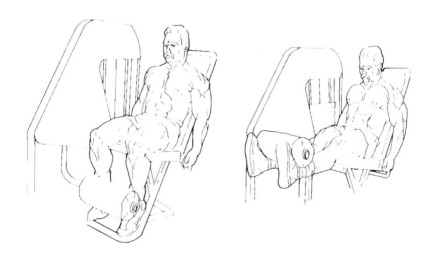

LEG PRESS

Muscles Involved: The gluteus maximus, upper hamstrings, vastus lateralis, vastus medialis, vastus intermedius and rectus femoris.

Execution: Sit back into the leg press machine and place your feet on the pushing plate. Press the plate up and release the restraining handles.

1. Bend your knees and slowly lower the weight plate, bringing your knees to your chest; 2. Slowly press the weight plate back up until your legs are fully extended; 3. Repeat as required.

Miscellaneous: There are several leg press machines available which move along an angled or horizontal track. Regardless of the machine, the exercise should be performed in the same manner.

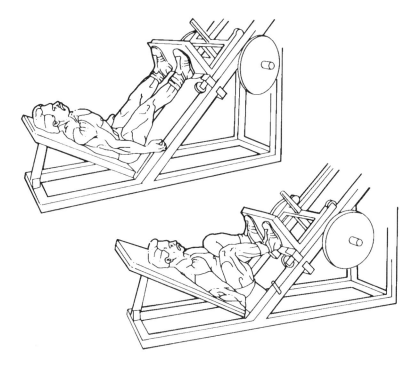

LUNGES

Muscles Involved: The vastus lateralis, vastus medialis, vastus intermedius, rectus femoris, gluteus maximus and hamstrings.

Execution: Assume a standing position with a barbell across the shoulders, your feet between hip- and shoulder-width apart.

1. Keeping your trunk in a upright position, step forward with a long stride lowering the body down and forward until the opposite knee lightly touches the floor; 2. Straighten the forward leg while bringing the rear leg up to meet it; 3. Repeat with the other leg; 4. Repeat as required.

Miscellaneous: Perform the exercise slowly concentrating on a full range of motion. When performing lunges for the first time, use a light weight until the technique is learned, then gradually increase the weight.

SQUAT

Muscles Involved: The vastus lateralis, vastus medialis, vastus intermedius, and rectus femoris.

Execution: Hold a barbell behind your neck with a grip wider than shoulder-width apart and stand with your feet shoulder-width apart. Point your toes slightly outward and distribute your body weight equally between both feet.

1. Keeping your head up and back straight, flex your knees and slowly lower yourself until your thighs are slightly lower than parallel with the floor; 2. Slowly straighten your legs keeping your head and chest up during the upward drive; 3. Repeat as required.

11
CALF
EXERCISES

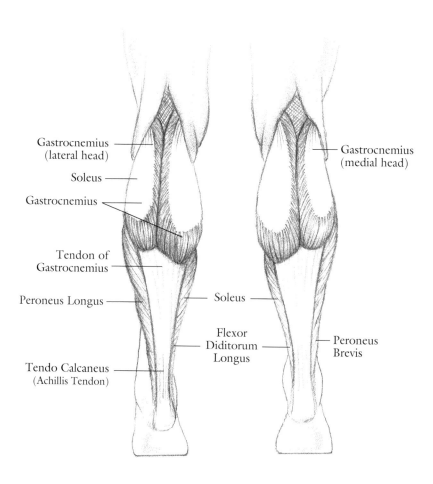

Gastrocnemius
(lateral head)

Soleus

Gastrocnemius

Tendon of
Gastrocnemius

Peroneus Longus

Tendo Calcaneus
(Achillis Tendon)

Gastrocnemius
(medial head)

Soleus

Flexor
Diditorum
Longus

Peroneus
Brevis

CALF RAISES

Muscles Involved: The gastrocnemius and soleus.

Execution: Stand erect with a barbell on your shoulders or a dumbbell in each hand. Place the balls of your feet on the edge of a 2-4 inch platform with your feet shoulder-width apart.

1. Slowly raise up on the balls of your feet as high as possible;
2. Slowly lower your feet beyond the starting position;
3. Repeat as required.

Miscellaneous: To involve and develop assisting muscles, change your foot position for each set. For example, point the toes inward or outward and place the feet wider or narrower.

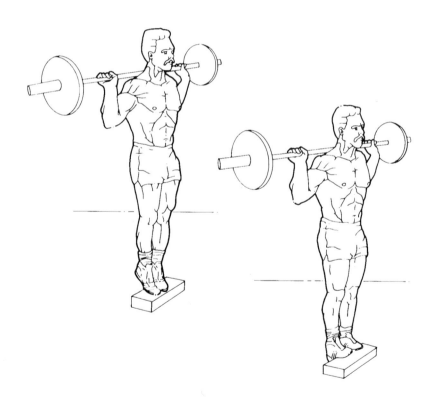

DONKEY CALF RAISES

Muscles Involved: The gatrocnemius and soleus.

Execution: Stand on the edge of a 2-4 inch platform with your heels extended over the edge. Bend over 90 degrees at the waist, supporting your upper body with a piece of exercise equipment. Have your training partner sit on your hips as far back as possible, keeping your legs straight and knees locked.

1. Slowly rise up on the balls of your feet as far as possible;
2. Slowly return to the starting position; 3. Repeat as required.

Miscellaneous: To increase the range of motion stand on a wooden block 1-4 inches high. Changing the position of your feet periodically will help develop assisting calf muscles. For example, point your toes in or out and/or place your feet at different widths.

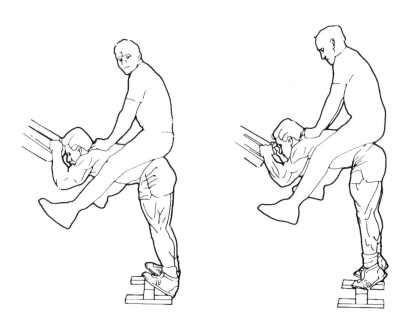

REVERSE CALF RAISES

Muscles Involved: The tibialis anterior.

Execution: Place your heels on a 2-4 inch block with your toes extended off the edge and support yourself with your hands.

1. Using your own body weight, slowly lower toes as far as possible; 2. Slowly raise your toes up as far as possible; 3. Repeat as required.

Miscellaneous: To increase the resistance have your training partner apply negative pressure.

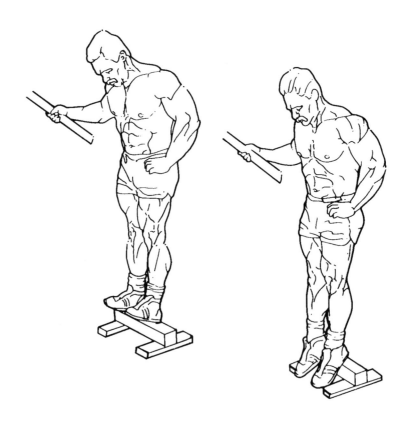

SEATED CALF RAISES

Muscles Involved: The gatrocnemius and soleus.

Execution: Sit on the calf machine with the balls of your feet on the floor bar and adjust the tip bar so the pads rest on your lower thighs. Your heels should be free to rise up and down.

1. Extend your ankles and raise up on the balls of your feet as high as possible; 2. Return to the starting position allowing your heels to go below the level of the balls of your feet; 3. Rise up again and repeat as required.

Miscellaneous: For greater calf development, hold your position on the top of the movement for several seconds. Changing foot positions will help develop assisting muscles used in this exercise. For example, point your toes in and out and change the width of your stance.

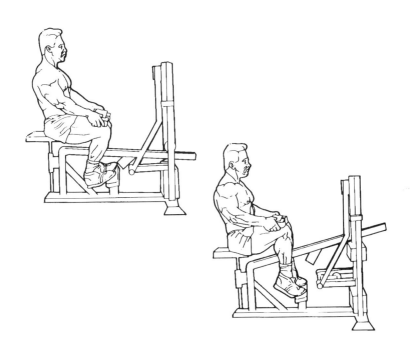

STANDING CALF RAISES

Muscles Involved: The gatrocnemius and soleus.

Execution: Step into a standing calf raise machine and place your shoulders under the pads. Bend your knees, positioning your toes on the block with your heels extended off the edge. Grasp the machine for support.

1. Slowly straighten your legs, keeping the knees slightly bent, then raise up on your toes as far as possible; 2. Slowly lower your heels toward the floor as far as possible; 3. Repeat as required.

Miscellaneous: To develop assisting muscles change your foot position. For example, point the toes inward or outward and place the feet wider or narrower.

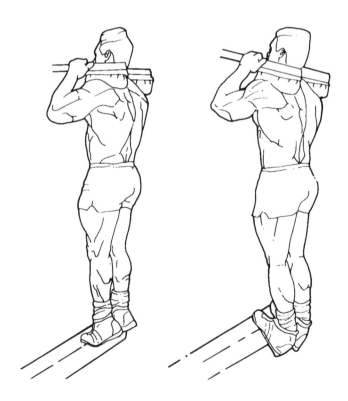

12
WEIGHT TRAINING RECORDS

Short-Term
Training Objectives

Long-Term
Training Objectives

Measurement Record

	Beginning	1st Month	Goal	2nd Month	Goal	3rd Month	Goal	4th Month	Goal	5th Month	Goal
Date											
Neck											
Shoulders											
Chest											
Upper Arm											
Forearm											
Waist											
Oblique											
Hips											
Upper Thigh											
Lower Thigh											
Calf											
Weight											
Height											
RHR											
% Fat											

146

Measurement Record

	6th Month	Goal	7th Month	Goal	8th Month	Goal	9th Month	Goal	10th Month	Goal	11th Month	Goal
Date												
Neck												
Shoulders												
Chest												
Upper Arm												
Forearm												
Waist												
Oblique												
Hips												
Upper Thigh												
Lower Thigh												
Calf												
Weight												
Height												
RHR												
% Fat												

Date _____ **Weight** _____ **Time** _____

Exercise	1		2		3		4		5		6	
	Rep	Wt	Rep	Wt	Rep	Wt	Rep	Wt	Rep	Wt	Rep	Wt

Notes: _____

Total Calorie Intake: _____ Protein Intake: _____ Carb. Intake: _____ Fat Intake: _____

Date _____ **Weight** _____ **Time** _____

Exercise	1		2		3		4		5		6	
	Rep	Wt	Rep	Wt	Rep	Wt	Rep	Wt	Rep	Wt	Rep	Wt

Notes:

Total Calorie Intake: _____ Protein Intake: _____ Carb. Intake: _____ Fat Intake: _____

Date _____ **Weight** _____ **Time**

Exercise	1		2		3		4		5		6	
	Rep	Wt	Rep	Wt	Rep	Wt	Rep	Wt	Rep	Wt	Rep	Wt

Notes:

Total Calorie Intake: _____   Protein Intake: _____   Carb. Intake: _____   Fat Intake: _____

Date _____ **Weight** _____ **Time** _____

Exercise	1		2		3		4		5		6	
	Rep	Wt	Rep	Wt	Rep	Wt	Rep	Wt	Rep	Wt	Rep	Wt

Notes: _____

Total Calorie Intake: _____ Protein Intake: _____ Carb. Intake: _____ Fat Intake: _____

Date _____   Weight _____   Time _____

Exercise	1		2		3		4		5		6	
	Rep	Wt	Rep	Wt	Rep	Wt	Rep	Wt	Rep	Wt	Rep	Wt

Notes: _____

Total Calorie Intake: _____   Protein Intake: _____   Carb. Intake: _____   Fat Intake: _____

Date _____ **Weight** _____ **Time** _____

Exercise	1 Rep	Wt	2 Rep	Wt	3 Rep	Wt	4 Rep	Wt	5 Rep	Wt	6 Rep	Wt

Notes: _____

Total Calorie Intake: _____ Protein Intake: _____ Carb. Intake: _____ Fat Intake: _____

Date _____ **Weight** _____ **Time** _____

Exercise	1 Rep	Wt	2 Rep	Wt	3 Rep	Wt	4 Rep	Wt	5 Rep	Wt	6 Rep	Wt

Notes: _____

Total Calorie Intake: _____ Protein Intake: _____ Carb. Intake: _____ Fat Intake: _____

Date _____ **Weight** _____ **Time** _____

Exercise	1		2		3		4		5		6	
	Rep	Wt	Rep	Wt	Rep	Wt	Rep	Wt	Rep	Wt	Rep	Wt

Notes: _____

Total Calorie Intake: _____   Protein Intake: _____   Carb. Intake: _____   Fat Intake: _____

Date _____ **Weight** _____ **Time** _____

Exercise	1 Rep	Wt	2 Rep	Wt	3 Rep	Wt	4 Rep	Wt	5 Rep	Wt	6 Rep	Wt

Notes: _____

Total Calorie Intake: _____   Protein Intake: _____   Carb. Intake: _____   Fat Intake: _____

Exercise

Date _____ **Weight** _____ **Time** _____

Exercise	1		2		3		4		5		6	
	Rep	Wt	Rep	Wt	Rep	Wt	Rep	Wt	Rep	Wt	Rep	Wt

Notes: _____

Total Calorie Intake: _____ Protein Intake: _____ Carb. Intake: _____ Fat Intake: _____

Exercise

	1	Rep	Wt	2	Rep	Wt	3	Rep	Wt	4	Rep	Wt	5	Rep	Wt	6	Rep	Wt

Date _____ **Weight** _____ **Time** _____

Notes: _____

Total Calorie Intake: _____ Protein Intake: _____ Carb. Intake: _____ Fat Intake: _____

Exercise

	1		2		3		4		5		6	
	Rep	Wt	Rep	Wt	Rep	Wt	Rep	Wt	Rep	Wt	Rep	Wt

Date _____ **Weight** _____ **Time** _____

Notes: _____

Total Calorie Intake: _____ Protein Intake: _____ Carb. Intake: _____ Fat Intake: _____

Date _____ **Weight** _____ **Time** _____

Exercise	1		2		3		4		5		6	
	Rep	Wt	Rep	Wt	Rep	Wt	Rep	Wt	Rep	Wt	Rep	Wt

Notes:

Total Calorie Intake: _____ Protein Intake: _____ Carb. Intake: _____ Fat Intake: _____

Exercise	1		2		3		4		5		6	
	Rep	Wt	Rep	Wt	Rep	Wt	Rep	Wt	Rep	Wt	Rep	Wt

Notes:

Total Calorie Intake: _____   Protein Intake: _____   Carb. Intake: _____   Fat Intake: _____

Date _____ **Weight** _____ **Time** _____

Exercise	1		2		3		4		5		6	
	Rep	Wt	Rep	Wt	Rep	Wt	Rep	Wt	Rep	Wt	Rep	Wt

Notes:

Total Calorie Intake: _____ Protein Intake: _____ Carb. Intake: _____ Fat Intake: _____

Date _____ Weight _____ Time _____

Exercise	1		2		3		4		5		6	
	Rep	Wt	Rep	Wt	Rep	Wt	Rep	Wt	Rep	Wt	Rep	Wt

Notes: _____

Total Calorie Intake: _____ Protein Intake: _____ Carb. Intake: _____ Fat Intake: _____

Date _____ **Weight** _____ **Time** _____

Exercise	1 Rep	Wt	2 Rep	Wt	3 Rep	Wt	4 Rep	Wt	5 Rep	Wt	6 Rep	Wt

Notes:

Total Calorie Intake: _____ Protein Intake: _____ Carb. Intake: _____ Fat Intake: _____

Date _____ **Weight** _____ **Time** _____

Exercise	1		2		3		4		5		6	
	Rep	Wt	Rep	Wt	Rep	Wt	Rep	Wt	Rep	Wt	Rep	Wt

Notes: _____

Total Calorie Intake: _____ Protein Intake: _____ Carb. Intake: _____ Fat Intake: _____

Date _____

Weight _____

Time _____

Exercise	1		2		3		4		5		6	
	Rep	Wt	Rep	Wt	Rep	Wt	Rep	Wt	Rep	Wt	Rep	Wt

Notes:

Total Calorie Intake: _____ Protein Intake: _____ Carb. Intake: _____ Fat Intake: _____

Date _____ **Weight** _____ **Time** _____

Exercise	1		2		3		4		5		6	
	Rep	Wt	Rep	Wt	Rep	Wt	Rep	Wt	Rep	Wt	Rep	Wt

Notes: _____

Total Calorie Intake: _____ Protein Intake: _____ Carb. Intake: _____ Fat Intake: _____

Date _____ **Weight** _____ **Time** _____

Exercise	1		2		3		4		5		6	
	Rep	Wt	Rep	Wt	Rep	Wt	Rep	Wt	Rep	Wt	Rep	Wt

Notes: _____

Total Calorie Intake: _____ Protein Intake: _____ Carb. Intake: _____ Fat Intake: _____

Date _____ **Weight** _____ **Time** _____

Exercise	1		2		3		4		5		6	
	Rep	Wt	Rep	Wt	Rep	Wt	Rep	Wt	Rep	Wt	Rep	Wt

Notes: _____

Total Calorie Intake: _____ Protein Intake: _____ Carb. Intake: _____ Fat Intake: _____

Date _____ Weight _____ Time _____

Exercise	1 Rep	Wt	2 Rep	Wt	3 Rep	Wt	4 Rep	Wt	5 Rep	Wt	6 Rep	Wt

Notes:

Total Calorie Intake: _____ Protein Intake: _____ Carb. Intake: _____ Fat Intake: _____

Date _____ Weight _____ Time _____

Exercise	1 Rep	Wt	2 Rep	Wt	3 Rep	Wt	4 Rep	Wt	5 Rep	Wt	6 Rep	Wt

Notes:

Total Calorie Intake: _____   Protein Intake: _____   Carb. Intake: _____   Fat Intake: _____

Date _____ **Weight** _____ **Time** _____

Exercise	1		2		3		4		5		6	
	Rep	Wt	Rep	Wt	Rep	Wt	Rep	Wt	Rep	Wt	Rep	Wt

Notes: _____

Total Calorie Intake: _____ Protein Intake: _____ Carb. Intake: _____ Fat Intake: _____

Date _____ **Weight** _____ **Time** _____

Exercise	1		2		3		4		5		6	
	Rep	Wt	Rep	Wt	Rep	Wt	Rep	Wt	Rep	Wt	Rep	Wt

Notes: _____

Total Calorie Intake: _____ Protein Intake: _____ Carb. Intake: _____ Fat Intake: _____

Exercise	1		2		3		4		5		6	
	Rep	Wt	Rep	Wt	Rep	Wt	Rep	Wt	Rep	Wt	Rep	Wt

Notes:

Total Calorie Intake: Protein Intake: Carb. Intake: Fat Intake:

Date _____ **Weight** _____ **Time** _____

Exercise	1		2		3		4		5		6	
	Rep	Wt	Rep	Wt	Rep	Wt	Rep	Wt	Rep	Wt	Rep	Wt

Total Calorie Intake: _____ Protein Intake: _____ Carb. Intake: _____ Fat Intake: _____

Notes: _____

Date _____ Weight _____ Time _____

Exercise	1		2		3		4		5		6	
	Rep	Wt	Rep	Wt	Rep	Wt	Rep	Wt	Rep	Wt	Rep	Wt

Notes: _____

Total Calorie Intake: _____ Protein Intake: _____ Carb. Intake: _____ Fat Intake: _____

Date _____ **Weight** _____ **Time** _____

Exercise	1		2		3		4		5		6	
	Rep	Wt	Rep	Wt	Rep	Wt	Rep	Wt	Rep	Wt	Rep	Wt

Notes: _____

Total Calorie Intake: _____ Protein Intake: _____ Carb. Intake: _____ Fat Intake: _____

Date _____ Weight _____ Time _____

Exercise

Exercise	1		2		3		4		5		6	
	Rep	Wt	Rep	Wt	Rep	Wt	Rep	Wt	Rep	Wt	Rep	Wt

Notes:

Total Calorie Intake: _____ Protein Intake: _____ Carb. Intake: _____ Fat Intake: _____

Date _____ **Weight** _____ **Time** _____

Exercise	1		2		3		4		5		6	
	Rep	Wt	Rep	Wt	Rep	Wt	Rep	Wt	Rep	Wt	Rep	Wt

Notes: _____

Total Calorie Intake: _____   Protein Intake: _____   Carb. Intake: _____   Fat Intake: _____

Date _____ **Weight** _____ **Time** _____

Exercise	1		2		3		4		5		6	
	Rep	Wt	Rep	Wt	Rep	Wt	Rep	Wt	Rep	Wt	Rep	Wt

Notes:

Total Calorie Intake: _____ Protein Intake: _____ Carb. Intake: _____ Fat Intake: _____

Date _____ Weight _____ Time _____

Exercise	1		2		3		4		5		6	
	Rep	Wt	Rep	Wt	Rep	Wt	Rep	Wt	Rep	Wt	Rep	Wt

Notes: _____

Total Calorie Intake: _____   Protein Intake: _____   Carb. Intake: _____   Fat Intake: _____

Date _____ **Weight** _____ **Time** _____

Exercise	1		2		3		4		5		6	
	Rep	Wt	Rep	Wt	Rep	Wt	Rep	Wt	Rep	Wt	Rep	Wt

Notes: _____

Total Calorie Intake: _____ Protein Intake: _____ Carb. Intake: _____ Fat Intake: _____

Exercise

Date		Weight			Time	

Exercise	1		2		3		4		5		6	
	Rep	Wt	Rep	Wt	Rep	Wt	Rep	Wt	Rep	Wt	Rep	Wt

Notes: _____

Total Calorie Intake: _____ Protein Intake: _____ Carb. Intake: _____ Fat Intake: _____

Date _____ **Weight** _____ **Time** _____

Exercise	1		2		3		4		5		6	
	Rep	Wt	Rep	Wt	Rep	Wt	Rep	Wt	Rep	Wt	Rep	Wt

Notes: _____

Total Calorie Intake: _____ Protein Intake: _____ Carb. Intake: _____ Fat Intake: _____

Date _____ **Weight** _____ **Time** _____

Exercise	1 Rep	Wt	2 Rep	Wt	3 Rep	Wt	4 Rep	Wt	5 Rep	Wt	6 Rep	Wt

Notes:

Total Calorie Intake: _____ Protein Intake: _____ Carb. Intake: _____ Fat Intake: _____

Date _____ Weight _____ Time _____

Exercise	1		2		3		4		5		6	
	Rep	Wt	Rep	Wt	Rep	Wt	Rep	Wt	Rep	Wt	Rep	Wt

Notes: _____

Total Calorie Intake: _____ Protein Intake: _____ Carb. Intake: _____ Fat Intake: _____

Date _____ **Weight** _____ **Time** _____

Exercise	1		2		3		4		5		6	
	Rep	Wt	Rep	Wt	Rep	Wt	Rep	Wt	Rep	Wt	Rep	Wt

Notes: _____

Total Calorie Intake: _____ Protein Intake: _____ Carb. Intake: _____ Fat Intake: _____

Date _____ Weight _____ Time _____

Exercise	1		2		3		4		5		6	
	Rep	Wt	Rep	Wt	Rep	Wt	Rep	Wt	Rep	Wt	Rep	Wt

Notes: _____

Total Calorie Intake: _____ Protein Intake: _____ Carb. Intake: _____ Fat Intake: _____

Date _____ Weight _____ Time _____

Exercise	1 Rep	Wt	2 Rep	Wt	3 Rep	Wt	4 Rep	Wt	5 Rep	Wt	6 Rep	Wt

Notes: _____

Total Calorie Intake: _____ Protein Intake: _____ Carb. Intake: _____ Fat Intake: _____

Date _____ **Weight** _____ **Time**

Exercise	1 Rep	Wt	2 Rep	Wt	3 Rep	Wt	4 Rep	Wt	5 Rep	Wt	6 Rep	Wt

Notes: _____

Total Calorie Intake: _____ Protein Intake: _____ Carb. Intake: _____ Fat Intake: _____

Date _____ **Weight** _____ **Time** _____

Exercise	1		2		3		4		5		6	
	Rep	Wt	Rep	Wt	Rep	Wt	Rep	Wt	Rep	Wt	Rep	Wt

Notes: _____

Total Calorie Intake: _____ Protein Intake: _____ Carb. Intake: _____ Fat Intake: _____

Date _____ **Weight** _____ **Time** _____

Exercise	1		2		3		4		5		6	
	Rep	Wt	Rep	Wt	Rep	Wt	Rep	Wt	Rep	Wt	Rep	Wt

Notes: _____

Total Calorie Intake: _____   Protein Intake: _____   Carb. Intake: _____   Fat Intake: _____

Exercise

	Date _____			Weight _____					Time _____			
	1		2		3		4		5		6		
	Rep	Wt	Rep	Wt	Rep	Wt	Rep	Wt	Rep	Wt	Rep	Wt

Notes: _____

Total Calorie Intake: _____ Protein Intake: _____ Carb. Intake: _____ Fat Intake: _____

Date _____ Weight _____ Time

Exercise	1		2		3		4		5		6	
	Rep	Wt	Rep	Wt	Rep	Wt	Rep	Wt	Rep	Wt	Rep	Wt

Notes: _____

Total Calorie Intake: _____ Protein Intake: _____ Carb. Intake: _____ Fat Intake: _____

Date _____ **Weight** _____ **Time** _____

Exercise	1		2		3		4		5		6	
	Rep	Wt	Rep	Wt	Rep	Wt	Rep	Wt	Rep	Wt	Rep	Wt

Notes: _____

Total Calorie Intake: _____ Protein Intake: _____ Carb. Intake: _____ Fat Intake: _____

Exercise

Date _____ **Weight** _____ **Time** _____

Exercise	1		2		3		4		5		6	
	Rep	Wt	Rep	Wt	Rep	Wt	Rep	Wt	Rep	Wt	Rep	Wt

Notes:

Total Calorie Intake: _____ Protein Intake: _____ Carb. Intake: _____ Fat Intake: _____

Date _____ **Weight** _____ **Time** _____

Exercise

	1		2		3		4		5		6	
	Rep	Wt	Rep	Wt	Rep	Wt	Rep	Wt	Rep	Wt	Rep	Wt

Notes:

Total Calorie Intake: _____ Protein Intake: _____ Carb. Intake: _____ Fat Intake: _____

Date _____ Weight _____ Time _____

Exercise	1		2		3		4		5		6	
	Rep	Wt	Rep	Wt	Rep	Wt	Rep	Wt	Rep	Wt	Rep	Wt

Notes: _____

Total Calorie Intake: _____   Protein Intake: _____   Carb. Intake: _____   Fat Intake: _____

Date _____ Weight _____ Time _____

Exercise	1 Rep	Wt	2 Rep	Wt	3 Rep	Wt	4 Rep	Wt	5 Rep	Wt	6 Rep	Wt

Notes:

Total Calorie Intake: _____ Protein Intake: _____ Carb. Intake: _____ Fat Intake: _____

Date _____ Weight _____ Time _____

Exercise	1		2		3		4		5		6	
	Rep	Wt	Rep	Wt	Rep	Wt	Rep	Wt	Rep	Wt	Rep	Wt

Notes: _____

Total Calorie Intake: _____   Protein Intake: _____   Carb. Intake: _____   Fat Intake: _____

Date _____ **Weight** _____ **Time** _____

Exercise	1		2		3		4		5		6	
	Rep	Wt	Rep	Wt	Rep	Wt	Rep	Wt	Rep	Wt	Rep	Wt

Notes: _____

Total Calorie Intake: _____ Protein Intake: _____ Carb. Intake: _____ Fat Intake: _____

Date _____ Weight _____ Time _____

Exercise	1		2		3		4		5		6	
	Rep	Wt	Rep	Wt	Rep	Wt	Rep	Wt	Rep	Wt	Rep	Wt

Notes: _____

Total Calorie Intake: _____   Protein Intake: _____   Carb. Intake: _____   Fat Intake: _____

Date _____ **Weight** _____ **Time** _____

Exercise	1		2		3		4		5		6	
	Rep	Wt	Rep	Wt	Rep	Wt	Rep	Wt	Rep	Wt	Rep	Wt

Notes: _____

Total Calorie Intake: _____   Protein Intake: _____   Carb. Intake: _____   Fat Intake: _____

Date _____ **Weight** _____ **Time** _____

Exercise	1		2		3		4		5		6	
	Rep	Wt	Rep	Wt	Rep	Wt	Rep	Wt	Rep	Wt	Rep	Wt

Notes: _____

Total Calorie Intake: _____ Protein Intake: _____ Carb. Intake: _____ Fat Intake: _____

Date _____ Weight _____ Time _____

Exercise	1		2		3		4		5		6	
	Rep	Wt	Rep	Wt	Rep	Wt	Rep	Wt	Rep	Wt	Rep	Wt

Notes: _____

Total Calorie Intake: _____ Protein Intake: _____ Carb. Intake: _____ Fat Intake: _____

Date _____ Weight _____ Time _____

Exercise	1 Rep	Wt	2 Rep	Wt	3 Rep	Wt	4 Rep	Wt	5 Rep	Wt	6 Rep	Wt

Notes:

Total Calorie Intake: _____ Protein Intake: _____ Carb. Intake: _____ Fat Intake: _____

Date _____ **Weight** _____ **Time** _____

Exercise	1		2		3		4		5		6	
	Rep	Wt	Rep	Wt	Rep	Wt	Rep	Wt	Rep	Wt	Rep	Wt

Notes: _____

Total Calorie Intake: _____ Protein Intake: _____ Carb. Intake: _____ Fat Intake: _____

Date _____ Weight _____ Time _____

| Exercise | 1 | | 2 | | 3 | | 4 | | 5 | | 6 | |
	Rep	Wt	Rep	Wt	Rep	Wt	Rep	Wt	Rep	Wt	Rep	Wt

Notes: _____

Total Calorie Intake: _____   Protein Intake: _____   Carb. Intake: _____   Fat Intake: _____

Exercise

Date _____ **Weight** _____ **Time** _____

Exercise	1		2		3		4		5		6	
	Rep	Wt	Rep	Wt	Rep	Wt	Rep	Wt	Rep	Wt	Rep	Wt

Notes: _____

Total Calorie Intake: _____ Protein Intake: _____ Carb. Intake: _____ Fat Intake: _____

Exercise

Date _____			Weight _____						Time _____					

Exercise	1 Rep	Wt	2 Rep	Wt	3 Rep	Wt	4 Rep	Wt	5 Rep	Wt	6 Rep	Wt

Notes:

Total Calorie Intake: _____   Protein Intake: _____   Carb. Intake: _____   Fat Intake: _____

Date _____ Weight _____ Time _____

Exercise	1		2		3		4		5		6	
	Rep	Wt	Rep	Wt	Rep	Wt	Rep	Wt	Rep	Wt	Rep	Wt

Notes: _____

Total Calorie Intake: _____ Protein Intake: _____ Carb. Intake: _____ Fat Intake: _____

Date _____ Weight _____ Time _____

Exercise	1 Rep	Wt	2 Rep	Wt	3 Rep	Wt	4 Rep	Wt	5 Rep	Wt	6 Rep	Wt

Notes:

Total Calorie Intake: _____ Protein Intake: _____ Carb. Intake: _____ Fat Intake: _____

Date _____   Weight _____   Time _____

Exercise	1 Rep	Wt	2 Rep	Wt	3 Rep	Wt	4 Rep	Wt	5 Rep	Wt	6 Rep	Wt

Notes:

Total Calorie Intake: Protein Intake: Carb. Intake: Fat Intake:

Date _____ **Weight** _____ **Time** _____

Exercise	1		2		3		4		5		6	
	Rep	Wt	Rep	Wt	Rep	Wt	Rep	Wt	Rep	Wt	Rep	Wt

Notes: _____

Total Calorie Intake: _____ Protein Intake: _____ Carb. Intake: _____ Fat Intake: _____

Exercise

Date _____ Weight _____ Time _____

Exercise	1		2		3		4		5		6	
	Rep	Wt	Rep	Wt	Rep	Wt	Rep	Wt	Rep	Wt	Rep	Wt

Notes:

Total Calorie Intake: _____ Protein Intake: _____ Carb. Intake: _____ Fat Intake: _____

Date _____ Weight _____ Time _____

Exercise	1		2		3		4		5		6	
	Rep	Wt	Rep	Wt	Rep	Wt	Rep	Wt	Rep	Wt	Rep	Wt

Notes:

Total Calorie Intake: _____ Protein Intake: _____ Carb. Intake: _____ Fat Intake: _____

Date _____ Weight _____ Time _____

Exercise	1		2		3		4		5		6	
	Rep	Wt	Rep	Wt	Rep	Wt	Rep	Wt	Rep	Wt	Rep	Wt

Notes: _____

Total Calorie Intake: _____ Protein Intake: _____ Carb. Intake: _____ Fat Intake: _____

Date _____ **Weight** _____ **Time** _____

Exercise	1		2		3		4		5		6	
	Rep	Wt	Rep	Wt	Rep	Wt	Rep	Wt	Rep	Wt	Rep	Wt

Notes: _____

Total Calorie Intake: _____   Protein Intake: _____   Carb. Intake: _____   Fat Intake: _____

Date _____ **Weight** _____ **Time** _____

Exercise	1		2		3		4		5		6	
	Rep	Wt	Rep	Wt	Rep	Wt	Rep	Wt	Rep	Wt	Rep	Wt

Notes: _____

Total Calorie Intake: _____ Protein Intake: _____ Carb. Intake: _____ Fat Intake: _____

Date _____ **Weight** _____ **Time** _____

Exercise	1		2		3		4		5		6	
	Rep	Wt	Rep	Wt	Rep	Wt	Rep	Wt	Rep	Wt	Rep	Wt

Notes: _____

Total Calorie Intake: _____ Protein Intake: _____ Carb. Intake: _____ Fat Intake: _____

Exercise

Date _____ **Weight** _____ **Time** _____

Exercise	1		2		3		4		5		6	
	Rep	Wt	Rep	Wt	Rep	Wt	Rep	Wt	Rep	Wt	Rep	Wt

Notes: _____

Total Calorie Intake: _____ Protein Intake: _____ Carb. Intake: _____ Fat Intake: _____

Date _____ **Weight** _____ **Time** _____

Exercise	1		2		3		4		5		6	
	Rep	Wt	Rep	Wt	Rep	Wt	Rep	Wt	Rep	Wt	Rep	Wt

Notes: _____

Total Calorie Intake: _____ Protein Intake: _____ Carb. Intake: _____ Fat Intake: _____

Date _____ **Weight** _____ **Time** _____

Exercise	1		2		3		4		5		6	
	Rep	Wt	Rep	Wt	Rep	Wt	Rep	Wt	Rep	Wt	Rep	Wt

Notes:

Total Calorie Intake: _____   Protein Intake: _____   Carb. Intake: _____   Fat Intake: _____

Date _____ Weight _____ Time _____

Exercise	1		2		3		4		5		6	
	Rep	Wt	Rep	Wt	Rep	Wt	Rep	Wt	Rep	Wt	Rep	Wt

Notes: _____

Total Calorie Intake: _____ Protein Intake: _____ Carb. Intake: _____ Fat Intake: _____

Exercise

Exercise	1 Rep	Wt	2 Rep	Wt	3 Rep	Wt	4 Rep	Wt	5 Rep	Wt	6 Rep	Wt

Date _____ Weight _____ Time _____

Notes: _____

Total Calorie Intake: _____ Protein Intake: _____ Carb. Intake: _____ Fat Intake: _____

Date _____ **Weight** _____ **Time** _____

Exercise

Exercise	1		2		3		4		5		6	
	Rep	Wt	Rep	Wt	Rep	Wt	Rep	Wt	Rep	Wt	Rep	Wt

Notes:

Total Calorie Intake: _____ Protein Intake: _____ Carb. Intake: _____ Fat Intake: _____

Date _____   Weight _____   Time _____

Exercise	1		2		3		4		5		6	
	Rep	Wt	Rep	Wt	Rep	Wt	Rep	Wt	Rep	Wt	Rep	Wt

Notes: _____

Total Calorie Intake: _____   Protein Intake: _____   Carb. Intake: _____   Fat Intake: _____

Date _____ Weight _____ Time _____

Exercise	1		2		3		4		5		6	
	Rep	Wt	Rep	Wt	Rep	Wt	Rep	Wt	Rep	Wt	Rep	Wt

Notes:

Total Calorie Intake: _____   Protein Intake: _____   Carb. Intake: _____   Fat Intake: _____

Date _____ Weight _____ Time _____

Exercise	1		2		3		4		5		6	
	Rep	Wt	Rep	Wt	Rep	Wt	Rep	Wt	Rep	Wt	Rep	Wt

Notes: _____

Total Calorie Intake: _____ Protein Intake: _____ Carb. Intake: _____ Fat Intake: _____

Date _____ **Weight** _____ **Time** _____

Exercise	1	Rep	Wt	2	Rep	Wt	3	Rep	Wt	4	Rep	Wt	5	Rep	Wt	6	Rep	Wt

Notes: _____

Total Calorie Intake: _____   Protein Intake: _____   Carb. Intake: _____   Fat Intake: _____

Date _____ **Weight** _____ **Time** _____

Exercise	1		2		3		4		5		6	
	Rep	Wt	Rep	Wt	Rep	Wt	Rep	Wt	Rep	Wt	Rep	Wt

Notes: _____

Total Calorie Intake: _____ Protein Intake: _____ Carb. Intake: _____ Fat Intake: _____

Date _____ Weight _____ Time _____

Exercise	1 Rep	Wt	2 Rep	Wt	3 Rep	Wt	4 Rep	Wt	5 Rep	Wt	6 Rep	Wt

Notes: _____

Total Calorie Intake: _____ Protein Intake: _____ Carb. Intake: _____ Fat Intake: _____

Exercise

Date _____ **Weight** _____ **Time** _____

Exercise	1 Rep	Wt	2 Rep	Wt	3 Rep	Wt	4 Rep	Wt	5 Rep	Wt	6 Rep	Wt

Notes: _____

Total Calorie Intake: _____ Protein Intake: _____ Carb. Intake: _____ Fat Intake: _____

Date _____ Weight _____ Time _____

Exercise	1	Rep	Wt	2	Rep	Wt	3	Rep	Wt	4	Rep	Wt	5	Rep	Wt	6	Rep	Wt

Notes: _____

Total Calorie Intake: _____ Protein Intake: _____ Carb. Intake: _____ Fat Intake: _____

Date _____ **Weight** _____ **Time** _____

Exercise

Exercise	1		2		3		4		5		6	
	Rep	Wt	Rep	Wt	Rep	Wt	Rep	Wt	Rep	Wt	Rep	Wt

Notes:

Total Calorie Intake: _____ Protein Intake: _____ Carb. Intake: _____ Fat Intake: _____

Date _____ **Weight** _____ **Time** _____

Exercise	1	Rep	Wt	2	Rep	Wt	3	Rep	Wt	4	Rep	Wt	5	Rep	Wt	6	Rep	Wt

Notes: _____

Total Calorie Intake: _____ Protein Intake: _____ Carb. Intake: _____ Fat Intake: _____

Exercise

Date _____ **Weight** _____ **Time** _____

Exercise	1	Wt	Rep	2	Wt	Rep	3	Wt	Rep	4	Wt	Rep	5	Wt	Rep	6	Wt	Rep	Wt

Notes: _____

Total Calorie Intake: _____ Protein Intake: _____ Carb. Intake: _____ Fat Intake: _____

Date _____ Weight _____ Time _____

Exercise

	1		2		3		4		5		6	
	Rep	Wt	Rep	Wt	Rep	Wt	Rep	Wt	Rep	Wt	Rep	Wt

Notes: _____

Total Calorie Intake: _____ Protein Intake: _____ Carb. Intake: _____ Fat Intake: _____

Date _____ **Weight** _____ **Time** _____

Exercise	1	Rep	Wt	2	Rep	Wt	3	Rep	Wt	4	Rep	Wt	5	Rep	Wt	6	Rep	Wt

Notes: _____

Total Calorie Intake: _____   Protein Intake: _____   Carb. Intake: _____   Fat Intake: _____

Date _____ Weight _____ Time _____

Exercise	1		2		3		4		5		6	
	Rep	Wt	Rep	Wt	Rep	Wt	Rep	Wt	Rep	Wt	Rep	Wt

Notes: _____

Total Calorie Intake: _____ Protein Intake: _____ Carb. Intake: _____ Fat Intake: _____

Date _____ **Weight** _____ **Time** _____

Exercise	1	Rep	Wt	2	Rep	Wt	3	Rep	Wt	4	Rep	Wt	5	Rep	Wt	6	Rep	Wt

Notes: _____

Total Calorie Intake: _____ Protein Intake: _____ Carb. Intake: _____ Fat Intake: _____

Date _____   **Weight** _____   **Time** _____

Exercise	1		2		3		4		5		6	
	Rep	Wt	Rep	Wt	Rep	Wt	Rep	Wt	Rep	Wt	Rep	Wt

Notes: _____

Total Calorie Intake: _____   Protein Intake: _____   Carb. Intake: _____   Fat Intake: _____

Date _____ **Weight** _____ **Time** _____

Exercise	1		2		3		4		5		6	
	Rep	Wt	Rep	Wt	Rep	Wt	Rep	Wt	Rep	Wt	Rep	Wt

Notes:

Total Calorie Intake: _____ Protein Intake: _____ Carb. Intake: _____ Fat Intake: _____

Date _____ **Weight** _____ **Time** _____

Exercise	1	Wt	Rep	2	Wt	Rep	3	Wt	Rep	4	Wt	Rep	5	Wt	Rep	6	Wt	Rep

Notes: _____

Total Calorie Intake: _____ **Protein Intake:** _____ **Carb. Intake:** _____ **Fat Intake:** _____

KINESIOLOGY OF EXERCISE

By Dr. Michael Yessis, Ph.D.

The most innovative book available on bodybuilding and general fitness weight training exercises and their variations.

Describing seventy exercises designed to tone, shape, and develop the body, "Kinesiology of Exercise" is more than a simple "How-To" manual. It includes:

- The sports in which each exercise will be a direct benefit.

- Photographs and drawings display how each exercise is correctly performed for maximum effectiveness and safety, and also what happens when an exercise is performed incorrectly.

- An in-depth biomechanical and kinesiological analysis of each exercise, written in a simple, easy-to-understand manner. Drawings illustrate the muscles and muscular interactions with the joints and limb changes involved in each exercise.

Dr. Michael Yessis is a biomechanics and exercise specialist. He has served as a training technique consultant for Olympic and professional sports teams, including the L.A. Raiders, L.A. Rams, and the U.S. Men's Volleyball Team. He has also written over 2,000 articles on fitness and sports training.

"Kinesiology of Exercise" will take you deeper into understanding weight training exercises found in "The Weight Training Workbook."

$17.95 (Add $2.00 postage and handling.)

JBBA Publishing
P.O. Box 842 • Appleton, WI 54912 • 1-800-245-7897

Qty.		Price	Total
	THE WEIGHT TRAINING WORKBOOK by Jim Bennett	$12.95	$
	THE WEIGHT TRAINING RECORD by Jim Bennett	$9.95	$
	THE WEIGHT TRAINING CALORIE REGISTER	$7.95	$
	TWT CALORIE REGISTER REFILL	$5.95	$
	THE CALORIE REGISTER – FOR WOMEN ONLY	$7.95	$
	THE CALORIE REGISTER REFILL	$5.95	$
	KINESIOLOGY OF EXERCISE by Dr. Michael Yessis, Ph.D.	$17.95	$

U.S. Funds Only. Add $2.00 postage & handling for first item and $1.00 for each additional item. Wisconsin residents add 5% Sales Tax. For Priority Mail Include an additional $2.00.

JBBA Publishing
P.O. Box 842
Appleton, WI 54912
1-800-245-7897
WK 12, 11, 10, 9, 8

Name _____
Address _____
City/State/Zip _____
Telephone _____
VISA/MasterCard _____ Exp. _____

Allow 2-4 weeks. Satisfaction guaranteed or return for full refund.

....

Qty.		Price	Total
	THE WEIGHT TRAINING WORKBOOK by Jim Bennett	$12.95	$
	THE WEIGHT TRAINING RECORD by Jim Bennett	$9.95	$
	THE WEIGHT TRAINING CALORIE REGISTER	$7.95	$
	TWT CALORIE REGISTER REFILL	$5.95	$
	THE CALORIE REGISTER – FOR WOMEN ONLY	$7.95	$
	THE CALORIE REGISTER REFILL	$5.95	$
	KINESIOLOGY OF EXERCISE by Dr. Michael Yessis, Ph.D.	$17.95	$

U.S. Funds Only. Add $2.00 postage & handling for first item and $1.00 for each additional item. Wisconsin residents add 5% Sales Tax. For Priority Mail Include an additional $2.00.

JBBA Publishing
P.O. Box 842
Appleton, WI 54912
1-800-245-7897
WK 12, 11, 10, 9, 8

Name _____
Address _____
City/State/Zip _____
Telephone _____
VISA/MasterCard _____ Exp. _____

Allow 2-4 weeks. Satisfaction guaranteed or return for full refund.

....

Qty.		Price	Total
	THE WEIGHT TRAINING WORKBOOK by Jim Bennett	$12.95	$
	THE WEIGHT TRAINING RECORD by Jim Bennett	$9.95	$
	THE WEIGHT TRAINING CALORIE REGISTER	$7.95	$
	TWT CALORIE REGISTER REFILL	$5.95	$
	THE CALORIE REGISTER – FOR WOMEN ONLY	$7.95	$
	THE CALORIE REGISTER REFILL	$5.95	$
	KINESIOLOGY OF EXERCISE by Dr. Michael Yessis, Ph.D.	$17.95	$

U.S. Funds Only. Add $2.00 postage & handling for first item and $1.00 for each additional item. Wisconsin residents add 5% Sales Tax. For Priority Mail Include an additional $2.00.

JBBA Publishing
P.O. Box 842
Appleton, WI 54912
1-800-245-7897
WK 12, 11, 10, 9, 8

Name _____
Address _____
City/State/Zip _____
Telephone _____
VISA/MasterCard _____ Exp. _____

Allow 2-4 weeks. Satisfaction guaranteed or return for full refund.

Qty.		Price	Total
	THE WEIGHT TRAINING WORKBOOK by Jim Bennett	$12.95	$
	THE WEIGHT TRAINING RECORD by Jim Bennett	$9.95	$
	THE WEIGHT TRAINING CALORIE REGISTER	$7.95	$
	TWT CALORIE REGISTER REFILL	$5.95	$
	THE CALORIE REGISTER – FOR WOMEN ONLY	$7.95	$
	THE CALORIE REGISTER REFILL	$5.95	$
	KINESIOLOGY OF EXERCISE by Dr. Michael Yessis, Ph.D.	$17.95	$

U.S. Funds Only. Add $2.00 postage & handling for first item and $1.00 for each additional item. Wisconsin residents add 5% Sales Tax. For Priority Mail Include an additional $2.00.

JBBA Publishing
P.O. Box 842
Appleton, WI 54912
1-800-245-7897
WK 12, 11, 10, 9, 8

Name _____
Address _____
City/State/Zip _____
Telephone _____
VISA/MasterCard _____ Exp. _____

Allow 2-4 weeks. Satisfaction guaranteed or return for full refund.

Qty.		Price	Total
	THE WEIGHT TRAINING WORKBOOK by Jim Bennett	$12.95	$
	THE WEIGHT TRAINING RECORD by Jim Bennett	$9.95	$
	THE WEIGHT TRAINING CALORIE REGISTER	$7.95	$
	TWT CALORIE REGISTER REFILL	$5.95	$
	THE CALORIE REGISTER – FOR WOMEN ONLY	$7.95	$
	THE CALORIE REGISTER REFILL	$5.95	$
	KINESIOLOGY OF EXERCISE by Dr. Michael Yessis, Ph.D.	$17.95	$

U.S. Funds Only. Add $2.00 postage & handling for first item and $1.00 for each additional item. Wisconsin residents add 5% Sales Tax. For Priority Mail Include an additional $2.00.

JBBA Publishing
P.O. Box 842
Appleton, WI 54912
1-800-245-7897
WK 12, 11, 10, 9, 8

Name _____
Address _____
City/State/Zip _____
Telephone _____
VISA/MasterCard _____ Exp. _____

Allow 2-4 weeks. Satisfaction guaranteed or return for full refund.

Qty.		Price	Total
	THE WEIGHT TRAINING WORKBOOK by Jim Bennett	$12.95	$
	THE WEIGHT TRAINING RECORD by Jim Bennett	$9.95	$
	THE WEIGHT TRAINING CALORIE REGISTER	$7.95	$
	TWT CALORIE REGISTER REFILL	$5.95	$
	THE CALORIE REGISTER – FOR WOMEN ONLY	$7.95	$
	THE CALORIE REGISTER REFILL	$5.95	$
	KINESIOLOGY OF EXERCISE by Dr. Michael Yessis, Ph.D.	$17.95	$

U.S. Funds Only. Add $2.00 postage & handling for first item and $1.00 for each additional item. Wisconsin residents add 5% Sales Tax. For Priority Mail Include an additional $2.00.

JBBA Publishing
P.O. Box 842
Appleton, WI 54912
1-800-245-7897
WK 12, 11, 10, 9, 8

Name _____
Address _____
City/State/Zip _____
Telephone _____
VISA/MasterCard _____ Exp. _____

Allow 2-4 weeks. Satisfaction guaranteed or return for full refund.

Qty.		Price	Total
	THE WEIGHT TRAINING WORKBOOK by Jim Bennett	$12.95	$
	THE WEIGHT TRAINING RECORD by Jim Bennett	$9.95	$
	THE WEIGHT TRAINING CALORIE REGISTER	$7.95	$
	TWT CALORIE REGISTER REFILL	$5.95	$
	THE CALORIE REGISTER – FOR WOMEN ONLY	$7.95	$
	THE CALORIE REGISTER REFILL	$5.95	$
	KINESIOLOGY OF EXERCISE by Dr. Michael Yessis, Ph.D.	$17.95	$

U.S. Funds Only. Add $2.00 postage & handling for first item and $1.00 for each additional item.
Wisconsin residents add 5% Sales Tax. For Priority Mail Include an additional $2.00.

JBBA Publishing Name _____
P.O. Box 842 Address _____
Appleton, WI 54912 City/State/Zip _____
1-800-245-7897 Telephone _____
WK 12, 11, 10, 9, 8 VISA/MasterCard _____ Exp. _____

Allow 2-4 weeks. Satisfaction guaranteed or return for full refund.

....

Qty.		Price	Total
	THE WEIGHT TRAINING WORKBOOK by Jim Bennett	$12.95	$
	THE WEIGHT TRAINING RECORD by Jim Bennett	$9.95	$
	THE WEIGHT TRAINING CALORIE REGISTER	$7.95	$
	TWT CALORIE REGISTER REFILL	$5.95	$
	THE CALORIE REGISTER – FOR WOMEN ONLY	$7.95	$
	THE CALORIE REGISTER REFILL	$5.95	$
	KINESIOLOGY OF EXERCISE by Dr. Michael Yessis, Ph.D.	$17.95	$

U.S. Funds Only. Add $2.00 postage & handling for first item and $1.00 for each additional item.
Wisconsin residents add 5% Sales Tax. For Priority Mail Include an additional $2.00.

JBBA Publishing Name _____
P.O. Box 842 Address _____
Appleton, WI 54912 City/State/Zip _____
1-800-245-7897 Telephone _____
WK 12, 11, 10, 9, 8 VISA/MasterCard _____ Exp. _____

Allow 2-4 weeks. Satisfaction guaranteed or return for full refund.

....

Qty.		Price	Total
	THE WEIGHT TRAINING WORKBOOK by Jim Bennett	$12.95	$
	THE WEIGHT TRAINING RECORD by Jim Bennett	$9.95	$
	THE WEIGHT TRAINING CALORIE REGISTER	$7.95	$
	TWT CALORIE REGISTER REFILL	$5.95	$
	THE CALORIE REGISTER – FOR WOMEN ONLY	$7.95	$
	THE CALORIE REGISTER REFILL	$5.95	$
	KINESIOLOGY OF EXERCISE by Dr. Michael Yessis, Ph.D.	$17.95	$

U.S. Funds Only. Add $2.00 postage & handling for first item and $1.00 for each additional item.
Wisconsin residents add 5% Sales Tax. For Priority Mail Include an additional $2.00.

JBBA Publishing Name _____
P.O. Box 842 Address _____
Appleton, WI 54912 City/State/Zip _____
1-800-245-7897 Telephone _____
WK 12, 11, 10, 9, 8 VISA/MasterCard _____ Exp. _____

Allow 2-4 weeks. Satisfaction guaranteed or return for full refund.